Qualification in Crime Prevention

Status reports from various European countries

Eds.
Marc Coester, Erich Marks and Anja Meyer

With contributions by:
RADIM BUREŠ, DIETER BURSSENS, MARC COESTER, ANTON DVORŠEK, PAUL EKBLOM, DANIJELA FRANGEŽ, OTMAR HAGE-MANN, JIM HILBORN, SOHAIL HUSAIN, ANU LEPS, MICHEL MARCUS, ERICH MARKS, GORAZD MEŠKO, ANJA MEYER, CHARLOTTE B. VIN-CENT, LODE WALGRAVE, ELMAR WEITEKAMP

Forum Verlag Godesberg GmbH 2008

Bibliographic Information of Deutsche Bibliothek (The German National Library)

The German National Library registers this publication in the
German National Bibliography; for detailed bibliographic data
consult the Internet: **http://dnb.ddb.de**.

© Forum Verlag Godesberg GmbH,
Mönchengladbach.
All rights reserved.
Mönchengladbach 2008

Produced by: Books on Demand GmbH, Norderstedt
Printed in Germany

Print layout: Marc Coester
Copy-Editor: Lucie Hamdi

Cover design: Konstantin Megas, Mönchengladbach

ISBN 978-3-936999-46-4

Contents

Introduction

Until recently crime prevention has been considered of little importance in the training of practitioners in related disciplines. In Germany as well as throughout Europe, there is a lack of opportunities for basic training and professional development. It can be assumed however that the demand for qualified specialists and managers in crime prevention will increase. There is now therefore a lot of catching up to develop the structure and content of specialized training in crime prevention across all the fields of work.

It was the objective of the Beccaria-Center *Professional Training in Crime Prevention* to work on closing this gap. With the financial support of the AGIS-programme of the European Commission (2005-2007), the project was implemented by the Council of Crime Prevention of Lower Saxony (Lower Saxony Ministry of Justice). Eight EU-partner organisations from the following countries were involved in the project: Belgium, the Czech Republic, Denmark, United Kingdom, Estonia, France, Italy, and Slovenia. One of the key tasks of the Beccaria-Center was to develop a range of scientific, demand-oriented and professional qualification offers. These offers comprise the drawing up of a basic training programme and the development of an in-service advanced Master's programme. Both of these offers are to contribute to an enhancement of professional competence and an improvement in professional practice.

Essentially, the contributions to this book document an expert meeting that took place in Hanover in April 2007 within the context of the EU-project. This EU-partner meeting offered a platform for a European exchange of experience and information. During the two-day meeting, the following representatives of the project partners gave talks on and discussed the current status of basic training and advanced training in European crime prevention: Manuele Braghero (Chief of cabinet of the representative for institutional reform and relations with local authorities in Tuscany, Italy), Dr. Radim Bureš (Home Office, the Czech Republic), Professor Dr. Paul Ekblom (Central Saint Martins College of Arts and Design, Great Britain), Dr. Lars Rand Jensen (Chief Constable of Odense Police, Denmark), Anu Leps (Ministry of Justice, Estonia), Michel Marcus (European Forum for Urban Safety, France), Dr. Gorazd Meško (University of Maribor, Slovenia) as well as Professor Dr. Elmar Weitekamp (University of Leuven, Belgium). At the same time, Dr. Volkhard Schindler (Regional CID Baden-Württemberg), Professor Dr. Bernd-Dieter Meier (University of Hanover) and Professor Otmar Hagemann (University of Applied Sciences, Kiel) gave status reports on the situation in Germany. Dr. Sohail Husain (Analytica Consulting Services Limited, Hampshire, UK), an experienced trainer and community safety specialist, chaired the meeting.

This compilation of status reports from the various countries reflects the current situation of qualification in crime prevention. The contributions show that it is necessary to expand basic training and further professional development opportunities in crime prevention. They clearly demonstrate that, on the one hand, the demand for high quality and sustainable crime prevention is higher than ever and, on the other hand, there is a clear lack of such training offers in Germany and in Europe more widely.

Marc Coester, Erich Marks, Anja Meyer

Sohail Husain[1]

Crime Prevention: An Emerging Profession

Over the past 20 years crime prevention has increasingly come to be recognised as a distinctive specialist discipline and profession. Developments that contributed to this change include:
- a growing body of theoretical / practical knowledge
- the emergence of a more technical and precise vocabulary and language
- growing employment opportunities for generalists and specialists.

There are now across the EU a large number of people employed in public service with a responsibility for crime prevention or community safety. Many have this as their sole and full-time responsibility. For others it is part of their job.

Most of these people have taken on such roles without any significant training in this subject area. They may have other professional qualifications, but most had little or no crime prevention training before they took on their jobs.

Across Europe there are few other areas of public service where such a situation exists. Whether employed in social work, housing, corrections, children's services, teaching, nursing or youth work, there are qualifications that are recognised nationally, increasingly internationally, that give employers a clear indication of the level of learning and expertise an individual has attained.

This is not intended to be a criticism. Rather it is a reflection of the fact that crime prevention is only now becoming established as a distinct profession and it is only with that development that a need for recognised professional training and qualifications arises.

In response, a wide range of independent training providers in the public, private and non-profit sectors has emerged in an organic or *ad hoc* way. In the UK, for example, many different types of course are now available: part/full-time, 'uncredited', certificate, diploma, post-graduate and options within undergraduate courses. Providers compete for students and each offers its own version of crime prevention or its specialisms. There is little quality assurance of such training and there are few agreed standards that would give employers confidence about the level of competence such training achieves.

---

[1] Contact details: 46 Park Road, Chandlers Ford, Hampshire, SO53 2ES, UK. Tel office: +44 (0) 23 8025 3863. Tel mobile: +44 (0) 79 5132 8791. Email: sohail.husain@analytica-consulting.co.uk.

This somewhat chaotic situation has advantages and may be inevitable. Students have a choice and competition for students can encourage quality improvement, creativity and value-for-money as providers strive for an advantage.

But the downside is that workforce skill levels remain very variable and consequently much work that is done in the name of crime prevention does not make good use of scarce resources. Services, programmes and projects are initiated that for one reason or another do not achieve their intended outcomes. Problems may be inadequately diagnosed. Inappropriate responses may be selected. Actions may be poorly implemented. Effectiveness may not be monitored.

But there is growing recognition that we are entering a different era. If crime prevention is to develop as a profession with credibility and the competence to deliver quality services providing value-for-money, we need much better learning programmes that equip staff for such work.

That raises a number of questions:
Should the employment market be the main driver for provision of educational programmes?
What is the range of jobs at which learning programmes should be directed?
What knowledge and skills are needed for different types of job?
At what levels should learning programmes be provided (certificate, diploma, undergraduate, graduate)?
How can learning opportunities be provided for those people that have crime prevention as an adjunct to their main role?
What should be considered the basic or core syllabus for a crime prevention practitioner?
In addition to training for 'generalists', in what specialist areas is training most needed?

It must also be clear to an employer what knowledge and skills are provided by particular training programmes, and they must be able to assess whether each is appropriate for a particular job. Employers need to recognise and have confidence in the qualifications offered by prospective staff.

That means having learning programmes that are validated or accredited as meeting certain recognised standards for a professional qualification. But what should those standards be and which organisation or agency should have that responsibility?

In the UK, 'Sector Skills Councils' (SSC) work with different sectors of the economy to
- identify the current and future skills that employers need in their workforce
- engage with learning providers to ensure appropriate high quality learning programmes are offered to meet those needs
- link the acquisition of learning to reputable and valued qualifications.

SSC exist for various sectors of the economy, such as Construction, Creative & Cultural, Hospitality, Leisure & Tourism, Social Care, Children and Young People and Justice. But although the Justice SSC has provided frameworks for a range of professions (legal advice staff, probation staff, work in courts, etc), there has been relatively little done in the area of crime prevention. It is clearly an area in which further development needs to take place, including the setting of standards.

Moreover, those standards arguably not only need to be recognised at national level, but internationally too. Who would do that at EU level? Are there other similar thematic areas which provide a model?

These are some of the questions considered in the Beccaria Partner Meeting. The papers that follow provide a valuable overview of what is happening in many different countries and how these questions are being addressed. They show an expanding range of initiatives to provide training and other learning opportunities in diverse settings and formats for practitioners employed in many different roles. What is also remarkable is that the same challenges and issues arise repeatedly, irrespective of the national context. It is clear therefore that there is much to be gained from working together to find the best way forward.

Marc Coester, Erich Marks, Anja Meyer

The Beccaria-Center: Professional Training in Crime Prevention

Initial Situation

"Quality through Qualification" – this is the subject of the Beccaria programme. The Beccaria programme forms a "quality-umbrella" over two consecutive EU-projects. Under this roof there are the "Beccaria-Project Quality Management in Crime Prevention" (2003-2005) and its successor "Beccaria-Center: Professional Training in Crime Prevention" (2005-2007). Both projects were implemented by the Council for Crime Prevention of Lower Saxony in cooperation with a large number of European partner organisations and thanks to financial support from the AGIS-programme of the European Commission, Directorate-General Justice, Freedom and Security.

Within the context of the Beccaria-project, diverse measures have been carried out to provide the players in the field with the basic tools for achieving better quality. The provision of tools such as the Beccaria-Standards is an important step on the way to reviewing the effectiveness of crime prevention projects and thus to an enhanced quality orientation. However, these tools do not automatically represent a guarantee of quality. In order to ensure their practical applicability, the required conditions have to be in place. No quality without qualification!

Description of the Problem

Due to increased professional demands (keyword: concept of lifelong learning), the need for qualified specialists and managers in crime prevention will continue to increase in the field of work as well as in science. Any preparation for taking on specialist and executive tasks needs to include the imparting of diverse crime prevention knowledge (basic and specialist knowledge) on the one hand and of management competencies on the other. It seems necessary to establish a qualifying programme and a Master's programme since no special advanced training opportunities in crime prevention across all the related fields of work and institutions are in place yet. In order to meet the increasing demand for and the changing requirements of professional staff in the field of crime prevention, advanced training must be expanded. In this context, there are two major shortcomings that must be tackled in a structured and focused way. In the first place, there are deficits with respect to a basic training in crime prevention. In the second place, there is a lot of catching up to do in terms of the structure of a specialized interdisciplinary advanced training in crime prevention, taking into account the differing starting levels and needs of crime prevention specialists and managers across Europe.

A comprehensive advanced training offer in crime prevention is required that is characterized by being inter- and multidisciplinary, complex and varied, with considerable interchange, and that imparts specialist knowledge with a particular focus on the applicability of this knowledge and its relevance to practice, without neglecting the scientific context. All of this must be based on a notion of crime prevention, which places emphasis on society as a whole. Crime prevention has to be understood as a local, national and international task. It requires interdisciplinary, integrative knowledge as well as an integral approach. This calls for the interaction, cooperation, and networking of all the forces of society from a wide range of areas, such as governmental and non-governmental agencies, the health sector, business, the education system, legal authorities and the police. Prevention specialists are faced with a whole host of tasks and areas of knowledge and a wide range of topics on different levels. Consequently, qualifications have to be acquired in the context of theory and practice.

Knowledge transfer is the object of the project "Beccaria-Center: Professional Training in Crime Prevention". Within the framework of the project, the "Beccaria Qualifying Programme Crime Prevention" and an advanced application-oriented "Master's Programme Crime Prevention" were developed between 2005 and 2007.

Measures

In order to develop this advanced training offer and its curricula, various measures were implemented. This included a stocktaking of the existing Master's programmes in Germany, Europe and the world. To summarize the results: there are no programmes covering various fields of study and topics that impart comprehensive qualifications for the field of crime prevention and have an interdisciplinary and multidisciplinary orientation. With the objective of identifying the need and (potential) demand for such a advanced training and of obtaining ideas and suggestions for its design with respect to contents and methods, several empirical surveys were conducted. The result of this needs analysis was that on the one hand, such a advanced training offer must impart specialist knowledge; on the other, it must pay particular attention to ensuring the applicability and practical relevance of this knowledge, without neglecting the scientific context.

On the basis of the stock-taking and needs analysis, modules for a "Qualifying Programme Crime Prevention" and a "Master's Programme Crime Prevention" were developed. In 2006, the EU-partners stated their views on the developed modules in writing.

Four external experts (from science and practice) provided competent assistance during the development and implementation process of the "Qualifying Programme Crime Prevention". Involving these evaluators served the objective of continuously assuring and reviewing the quality of the work throughout the duration of the project.

With the same objective of assuring and reviewing the quality of the "Master's Programme Crime Prevention", the Zentrale Evaluations- und Akkreditierungsagentur (ZEvA) (Central Evaluation and Accreditation Agency) was involved. In cooperation with two experts they had appointed, their particular task was to act as consultants with respect to the study and examination regulations, the development of the curriculum and the module catalogue, including the objectives of the qualification.

The key **results** of the measures outlined above are firstly the "Beccaria Qualifying Programme Crime Prevention" and secondly the conception and documentation of the "Master's
programme Crime Prevention", including the examination regulations and the educational and
admission requirements.

The "Beccaria Qualifying Programme Crime Prevention"

As of February 2008, the Council for Crime Prevention of Lower Saxony is offering the
"Beccaria Qualifying Programme Crime Prevention". For the first time, all those who are active in fields relevant to crime prevention can take part in a targeted advanced training. The
comprehensive qualifying programme imparts basic knowledge in criminology, crime prevention, basic legal principles, research methods, and project and quality management. Accordingly, it comprises four consecutive modules: 1. Module Criminology, 2. Module Crime Prevention, 3. Module Project Management and 4. Module Practical Project Work.

On six weekends and four individual days there will be intensive attendance courses to impart
knowledge, apply and implement it. The competent lecturers have many years of teaching
experience at universities, universities of applied sciences and in adult education and are
crime prevention experts. Upon successful completion of the qualifying programme, the degree "Crime Prevention Specialist" will be awarded to the participants.

The programme offers the chance to expand professional competence in the context of an in-
service series of training courses with practical relevance, which increases the value and quality of the everyday work of those active in prevention. The teaching contents imparted can be
experienced and implemented in their daily work. On the one hand they are scientifically
sound, on the other hand they are of considerable relevance to practice and can be applied to
current professional issues. Thus, the increasing demand for (more) quality in practical crime
prevention work is taken into account.

The target group for the qualifying programme are mainly players with relevant experience in
the field of crime prevention (full-time, part-time or voluntary), managers of local councils,
prevention experts with governmental or municipal agencies and of independent agencies,
employees of public and private (social) services, of the legal authorities (probation services,
courts, prisons etc.), in the field of basic training and advanced training and schools.

The qualification goals include basic knowledge in criminology and crime prevention, legal
matters (children and youth assistance plan, juvenile criminal law, criminal law, law of criminal procedure, penal system) and basics of research methods, (project) management competences as well as inter- and multidisciplinary skills (networking).
With this qualification, action patterns in the daily crime prevention work are to be expanded
and strengthened. This includes:

- The development of preventive measures, consulting the most recent scientific findings and data;
- Critical assessment of specialist knowledge (articles in professional journals, book contents etc.);
- Reviewing the effectiveness of preventive measures (carrying out a before/after-comparison, knowledge of qualitative and quantitative procedures);
- Managing and chairing prevention committees and work groups;
- Management of projects (project management, PR-work, networking, etc.), including planning and organization of human, financial and material resources as well as fund-raising (sponsoring etc.).

Module "Criminology"

The module Criminology has the objective that the participants

- Have basic knowledge in the fields of Cognitive Science, Sociology of Knowledge, as well as Criminology;
- Are able to critically analyse scientific texts and theories;
- Are able to substantiate their respective point of view as observers, using reasoned arguments;
- Are capable of regarding *crime* as well as the system of Criminal Law as a social construction;
- Know the fundamentals of the history of Criminology and
- the most important basic concepts of Criminology;
- Are familiar with the most well known crime theories;
- Can distinguish methods of empirical criminological research and make use of them;
- Are able to make use of crime statistics (e.g. PKS) in crime-prevention work;
- Have gained an insight into criminological research on unreported delinquency.

Module "Crime Prevention"

After taking the module Crime Prevention, the participants should

- Know the basic concepts, their systemization and the essential meaning of crime prevention;
- Be able to play an informed role in local crime prevention networks;
- Be informed about the most important institutions, committees, structures in crime prevention;
- Have tackled selected subject areas of crime prevention and have become acquainted with current programmes, projects and research results;
- and be able to critically analyse and evaluate prevention measures, drawing on their experience and knowledge.

Module "Project Management"

After completing this module, the participants should be able to play an informed part in developing, implementing and evaluating prevention projects. This includes knowledge about

- Description and analysis of problems
- Survey instruments
- Weighing up risks
- Analyses of objectives
- Project preparations
- Project conceptions
- The system of objectives (basic-, framework-, end-result-, process- and structural objectives)
- Objective-setting and formulation of objectives
- Ways of carrying out projects
- Operationalisation of objectives
- Reporting system/minute-taking
- Controlling-tasks
- Concepts/methods of evaluation and documentation.

Module "Practical Project Work"

The objective of the Practical Project Work is to enable the participants to practically apply the learning results from the three preceding modules. The informed application refers to the development, implementation and analysis of a crime prevention project. Here the most important point is to support the new learning process in a reflexive manner and give guidance for actions. In this context, the measures include, for example, supervision, coaching, and consulting. Participants are to share practical experiences and to analyse results with respect to people and issues, to overcome obstacles, control the project phases, modify the objectives, measures and methods, discuss the project evaluation and present success and failure, personal experiences as well as consequences for future projects.

The qualifying programme will be offered at regular intervals. In principle, participants can take a module of their choice or all four modules. Upon successful completion of all four modules, participants are awarded the degree "Qualified Crime Prevention Specialist". Each individual module comprises two weekend courses per year and a total of 28 lessons. Additionally, there are about 20 hours of self-study. Further information is available at www.beccaria.de.

Master's Programme Crime Prevention

The **"Master's Programme Crime Prevention"** is an in-service, advanced and application-oriented programme. Since it qualifies for specialist and executive tasks, it is addressed to persons who aspire to executive positions in fields of practice related to crime prevention. The eligibility and admission requirements include a degree in Social Work, Education, Psychology, Sociology, Social Sciences, Law, Medicine, Police or Administrative Sciences and at least two years of work experience in a related field. The participants acquire a wide range of criminological and crime prevention knowledge, management competences an interdisciplinary and multidisciplinary skills. The programme is to prepare for taking over executive and managerial positions (e.g. with state prevention councils, committees of local crime prevention, regional CIDs or the Federal Criminal Police and comparable higher regional or federal authorities, with municipal and district administrations, with youth and social services, with universities of applied sciences, NGOs, independent agencies and in the business/industrial sector).

Accordingly, the competence goals include:
- The ability to analyse changes in society and to develop adequate prevention strategies;
- to develop measures, making use of scientific findings and data;
- to review the effectiveness of preventive measures (evaluation);
- to manage and chair prevention committees and work groups;
- to manage projects;
- to do PR-work;
- to offer expert consulting and support to decision-makers (in particular to those involved in politics and administration);
- to do cross-departmental and cross-institutional work (networking) as well as
- HR-planning, planning of advanced training, organisation and equipment, including fund-raising.

At present, in Germany it is not possible to acquire such a profile with a focus on crime prevention. There is no comprehensive offer for this.[2]

---

[2] Study programmes teaching important sub-areas of this context, are, for example, the advanced Master's programmes "Criminology and Police Sciences" of the Faculty of Law at the Ruhr-University Bochum (Chair for Criminology), "Deviance Management" at Lüneburg University, "Conflict Management and Violence Prevention" at the Hochschule für Soziale Arbeit & Diakonie (Protestant University for Social Work) Hamburg, "International Criminology" at the Institut für Kriminologische Sozialforschung (Institute for Criminological Social Research) Hamburg University, "Comparative Law and European Law" at Greifswald University, "Comparative and European Law" at Hanse Law School (Oldenburg, Bremen, Groningen), "Public Administration - Police Management" at the Polizeiführungsakademie (Academy for Police Executives) Münster as well as the Bachelor's programme "Safety Management" at the Fachhochschule für Verwaltung und Rechtspflege (University of Applied Sciences for Administration and Judicature) Berlin.

The students complete four modules within four semesters: 1. Criminology and Criminological Research Methods, 2. Crime Prevention, 3. Basic Legal Conditions of Prevention, 4. Organisational and Managerial Foundations of Prevention.

The modules and their teaching contents are described below:

The Module "Criminology and Criminological Research Methods"
- Unreported and recorded delinquency;
- Facts on delinquents and victims
- Crime and victimization according to age and gender, to city and rural areas, and to regional particularities;
- Criminological and victimological research methods;
- Opportunities and limitations of quantitative and qualitative data surveys;
- Case file analysis and biographical research as ways of gaining criminological insight;
- Procedure of evaluation to clarify the effectiveness of projects and programmes;
- Crime theories to explain deviant behaviour and the development of criminal careers;
- Psychologically, social-psychologically and sociologically oriented theories as well as supplementary integration concepts;
- The importance of family, school, peer group, drug abuse and use of mass media for the development of criminal careers;
- Migration and crime;
- The acceptance of notions of manliness that justify violence;
- Specific disadvantage and strain among migrants with respect to neighbourhood, domestic violence, education and social integration;
- Neighbourhood and crime;
- Criminal geography,
- Criminological aspects of homelessness;
- Social capital as a preventive factor;
- Corruption in public administration and in business;
- Conditions leading to white-collar crime;
- Social control of crime
- Forms and importance of informal control
- From reporting a crime to the execution of the verdict (police, public prosecutor's office, criminal courts, diversion);
- Social services in the criminal justice system (in particular court assistance in juvenile courts, court assistance, probation service, probationary supervision, victim-offender mediation); penal system, detention orders.

The Module "Crime Prevention"
1. Social-psychological key area
- Primary prevention by measures that prevent potential causes of crime from having an effect on children and young people;

- Measures for social integration of migrants in kindergartens and primary schools or programmes for the early detection of neglect in children;
- Measures to prevent domestic violence; e.g. local activities of the Kinderschutzbund (child protection agency), of the youth welfare office or other independent agencies of the youth services;.
- Advisory support offered in schools;
- Projects for local enforcement of the laws of protection against violence;
- Assistance at women's refuges;
- Crime prevention measures in schools, e.g. training pupils as mediators;
- Close cooperation between police and schools;
- Introduction of certain training and sensitization programmes;
- Measures to fight bullying;
- Anti-truancy measures, establishing all-day schools as a chance to expand the prevention approaches.

2. Technical-planning and socio-scientific key area:

- Technical prevention
- Measures to reduce opportunities for delinquency by improved lighting, alarm systems, technical anti-theft and burglary prevention devices and access controls;
- Increased safety in public places by means of video surveillance;
- Local crime prevention;
- Regional criminological analysis to measure the impact of crime in boroughs and municipalities, within districts and nationally as a basis for discovering settlement-specific causes of crime;
- Establishing local prevention councils, in which all the institutions are involved, which would like to take part in crime prevention work,
- Developing measures and long-term projects for crime prevention (for example by improving the social and school integration of children and young people from marginal groups of society);
- Continuous monitoring and scientific evaluation of local crime prevention measures;
- Organizing state prevention councils and the German Prevention Day as opportunities to exchange experiences with measures of (local) crime prevention, to promote the dialogue between research and practice and help international experience come into effect;
- Crime prevention through town and regional development planning that specifically counteracts impoverishment of certain parts of the towns.

3. Selected key areas of crime prevention:

- Prevention of corruption in public administration and in business (for example by establishing adequate control structures, transparency in awarding public funds, rotation of the officials in charge, appointment of a state ombudsman to act as a contact person for citizens, self-reporters and whistle-blowers; establishing a confi-

dential telephone line, creation of local cooperation structures to fight corruption in the local government);
- Specific and general prevention through measures of social crime control;
- The importance of the likelihood of sanctions or of their severity for general prevention;
- The influence of informal sanctions;
- The importance of the time factor in criminal proceedings; measures to accelerate criminal proceedings;
- Research findings on recidivism with respect to various educational measures and sanctions; the effect of social training courses and therapeutic treatment approaches with different groups of delinquents (young violent criminals, drug addicts, sex offenders).

Module "Basic Legal Conditions of Prevention"
- Youth assistance law and family law;
- Intervention possibilities by the state when the development of children and young people is at particular risk (for example when the best interests of a child are endangered, in the case of drug addiction, when people endanger themselves or others, e.g. so-called joyriders, truancy);
- Juvenile criminal law with emphasis on non-custodial measures;
- Criminal law; law of criminal procedure with emphasis on remand law; penal system with emphasis on measures to prepare inmates for their discharge.

Module "Organisational and Managerial Principles of Prevention"
- Organisation and management of local prevention councils;
- Field reports on the practice of such organisations;
- Project management of prevention measures;
- Fund-raising and public relations;
- Budgeting of prevention measures;
- Accounting and writing reports on the expenditure of funds;
- Cost-benefit analysis.

The participants acquire criminological and crime prevention knowledge, management competences and the ability to work on an interdisciplinary and multidisciplinary basis. The standard period of study is two years at 60 credit points (ECTS). A total of 600 hours is planned for the attendance phases. Additionally, a three-week intensive phase is offered once a year (240 hours of attendance), followed by a total of 40 weekend courses (360 hours of attendance). For the Master's thesis 450 hours are estimated and 750 hours for self-study. The examination system has an in-service orientation. In principle, one examination per module is offered.

The number of students accepted for the Master's programme per year should not exceed 25. Upon successful completion of the final examination, they are awarded the internationally recognized degree Master of Arts (M.A.). Currently, there are negotiations with universities on the possibility of introducing the Master's programme and to start the accreditation procedure.

Gorazd Meško, Danijela Frangež, Anton Dvoršek

Status Report Slovenia - Current Endeavours in Crime Prevention Training in Slovenia

The paper deals with the development of crime prevention training in Slovenia and especially with recent changes in the new study programmes at the Faculty of Criminal Justice and Security, following the Bologna recommendations and providing education for undergraduate and postgraduate students of Criminal Justice and Security. The authors will give a detailed presentation of study programmes related to crime prevention at the Faculty of Criminal Justice and Security. The content of the discussed study programmes is to be kept up to date with the fast development of knowledge in the fields of criminal justice, crime prevention and security as well as with trends in the relevant disciplines in Europe and throughout the world. The main goal of any new programme is to contribute to the body of international knowledge of criminal justice and security and educate specialists and experts in the fields of crime prevention, provision of safety/security and crime control.

Keywords: crime prevention, training, Slovenia

1. Introduction

Crime prevention is not a new concept. It began with victimization and people's desire for a safe life without a threat to themselves and their loved ones. The contemporary preventive measures are therefore only old practices building on and expanding the basic work of the past (Meško, 2002: 47).

Modern society has developed a fetish for security and a resistance to risks. This partly happened on account of groundless fears of crime and terrorism. In the last decade, the rising awareness and interests of researchers and experts in criminal justice, private security, politicians and the public in general, have led the way to crime prevention activities and the development of this field (Meško, 2000: 297).

Crime prevention is a general slogan used everywhere, irrespective of the diverse social factors related to it or professions dealing with it (Pečar, 2002: 4). To understand crime prevention and its meaning to society, the knowledge of social control, its forms and dimensions, is highly important. Social control, however, is a rather broad conception. It includes all the mechanisms, structures, institutions, systems, activities and phenomena that (re)create order in society (Kanduč, 2004: 4).

The line between crime repression and prevention is very thin. In some cases, crime prevention could easily be presented as repression, although the offences have not yet been committed. Prevention activities of the police are often so harsh that people are feeling victimized even before any crime happens. On the one hand innocent and on the other very repressive, (police) crime prevention measures could easily be transformed into refined "people-friendly" social control. Its nets are spread so quietly that people often consider them as something good and innocent, their true intention cannot be discovered and community surveillance could increase (Meško and Vogrinec, 2003: 1).

Anyhow, the efforts of the new criminal policy marked crime prevention as the main means in the fight against crime in areas, where the legal authorities proved to be insufficient; especially in more complex offences as organized crime, corruption, human trafficking, computer crime, state crime, and international terrorism. Crime prevention therefore appears to be an alternative, which is usually more humane, efficient and less expensive than repression. Its task is to motivate the potential victims to take care of their own safety. Crime prevention and provision of safety become more and more important, also in Slovenia, where the crime rate has been increasing continuously over the last 15 years (http://www.policija.si). Every day, the offences are taking new forms on all levels of society, and in many cases the offenders are more educated and skilled than the legal authorities. The recent crime prevention activities show that the main goal of preventive measures is (at least) to alleviate the consequences, or even to decrease the level of offences. To achieve this aim it is of utmost importance to know society and its changes very well (Kanduč, 2004: 3).

2. Crime Prevention in Slovenia

In late 80s, Slovenia presented a border between Western Europe and former Yugoslavia, but this geographic position had its own advantages. Slovenia was in the most favourable position for getting familiar with Western criminology and its advanced development.

After 1991, when Slovenia became an independent and autonomous country, the influence of the West became even more noted. The interest in Western crime prevention knowledge increased significantly. At first, the attention was merely theoretical, but later and especially in the present situation, the practice became important as well. There are many movements, programmes and campaigns that give instructions for better self-protection against different offences, also with respect to violence that is usually accepted as normal (even if it is not). Recent changes in Slovenia, however, call for new professionals who will be able to overcome "common sense" and responses to crime and disorder problems in local communities of Slovenia that come only from the police. Those new professionals will also play a more active role in local safety/security councils. These councils are still in the process of development (Meško and Lobnikar, in Meško, Bučar-Ručman, Tominc, and Maver, 2007: 236).

But this is only one part of crime prevention activities taking place in Slovenia. If we look further, we could find numerous strategies developed by repressive agencies (Meško, 2004: 3). The legal framework in Slovenia still requires a centralised approach to the solution of crime, safety/security and disorder problems. Some changes are being discussed and plans are being made for the future. The latest (admitted) documents on a crime prevention strategy are the National Crime Prevention and Crime Control Strategy of the Republic of Slovenia (National Gazette, 40/2007) and the Medium–Term Plan of Police Work for the Period 2003-2007 (www.policija.si).

The Slovenian territory is part of the most important transit route, also known as "crossroads of East and West", where different migration patterns are taking place. Consequently, the Slovenian border is crossed by different individuals and groups originating from Eastern countries such as Hungary, Romania, Slovakia, and from the countries of former Yugoslavia (Croatia, B&H, Serbia and FRYM). Many of these come to Slovenia with one particular aim: they want to commit various types of crime (Frangež, 2007). The police should be aware of this trend among foreign offenders; therefore they should adapt their work plan accordingly, also with respect to crime prevention, and establish a better international cooperation with foreign police organizations in the region and other institutions and organizations as well.

Private security organizations play a very important role in today's society. During the last few years their knowledge of situational prevention has improved; therefore the offer of technical protection could be even more advanced. The public is getting more and more familiar with their work, especially now that they have realized that the police cannot offer them sufficient security concerning crime prevention. This is why private security organizations are often ahead of the police regarding crime prevention. However, the involvement of private security is getting stronger every day. Their measures are strengthening crime prevention on the one hand; on the other hand, their activities in the environment increase people's feeling of safety. The future development of private security will be mainly in the field of technical improvements. Nevertheless, we shall not ignore the non-technical part of private security. Therefore, the training of security guards is important as well. Basic and advanced training of private security officers and managers should include the subjects of crime prevention, especially those of situational crime prevention and the crime prevention industry (Meško, 2007).

The discussion in different fields about more successful prevention work is of significant importance. Any subjects and organizations that are in any way involved with crime prevention strategies should be introduced, especially to the police. The police as the single body of law enforcement in Slovenia play a significant part in fighting crime. Their preventive activities could also be defined as "mainly paraprofessional, unprofessional and lay activity" (Pečar, 2002: 3). Therefore, it is very important to offer crime prevention training to police officers. Slovenian police officers receive such training in crime prevention/community policing as part of their basic police training (Rejc Buhovac, Savič, Kerševan, Pevcin and Meško, 2007). Several courses designed as an in-service training are also related to crime prevention and community policing (Meško, 2007). However, the preventive measures of the police must be in accordance with the law, which also defines the tasks the police have to perform.

The means, methods and initiatives of crime prevention are usually defined as chameleonic concepts that indicate that the same preventive measures could be understood and performed differently for different circumstances. One of many means can, according to some experts, also be imprisonment, provided the severe penalization is taking place soon after the offence has been committed. According to others, the practical methods of crime prevention have no relation to penology and law enforcement. Furthermore, crime prevention cannot be interpreted only as punishments of offenders, it is something "more" (Meško, 2002: 55-56). And what could we describe as "more"? Is that role assigned to situational prevention? In Slovenia police turn their attention mostly to situational prevention effects. Situational prevention is becoming more and more popular in Slovenia. Its directions are applied when building new and restoring old settlements. At the same time, the role of potential victims is also becoming important. Society should gain knowledge on how to ensure its own safety, regarding the most frequently committed offences, such as property and violent crimes. The prevention of violent crimes is highly delicate because the measures have to work in the domestic environment.

Police attention is therefore directed to the victims (Pečar, 2002: 1) and their own provision of safety. However, crime prevention is not only the responsibility of the police (Dvoršek, 2004: 260). The local communities, neighbourhoods and local authorities should provide better safety standards for their own community and pay much greater attention to increasing (formal) social control wherever possible, that could be discreetly preformed in combination with preventive measures of the police. This type of police activity could be successfully prevented by incorporating institutions and community representatives into agencies that define crime prevention priorities (Meško and Vogrinec, 2004: 1).

Crime prevention also has an important place in police measures to reduce crime. Their efforts are most (if at all) effective with respect to conventional crime. What about other types of crime? Especially crimes that usually go unnoticed when accomplished? Such types of crime, for example computer crime, are - despite their invisibility - very present in our everyday life. The security of electronic systems should, therefore, have our full attention. Nevertheless, information security is not alone on the way to becoming a notable discipline. Environmental crime is becoming a much discussed subject, in police forces as well.

Crime prevention in Slovenia, however, found its place also in literature and educational institutions. In Slovenia, the social control has been reflected upon in three monographs by Pečar[3]: *The Formal Social Control* (1988), *The Informal Social Control* (1991), and *The Institutionalized Informal Social Control* (1992). Furthermore, in September 2004 the National Criminological Conference: Crime Prevention – Theory, Practice & Dilemmas, took place at the Faculty of Law in Ljubljana. Some selected conference papers are presented also in the volume: *Crime Prevention – Theory, Practice & Dilemmas* (Meško, 2004) that is "especially designed for use as a key text for readers interested in crime prevention problems in contemporary Slo-

---

[3] All three monographs are in Slovenian.

venia". The volume was: "offered in tribute of Slovene theory and practice of crime prevention and criminologists, other social scientists and practitioners who have reflected upon crime prevention substantively. This collection consist of 42 papers in the following chapters: Conceptual Dilemmas of Crime Control, Analysis of Crime for the Purpose of Crime Prevention, Prevention of Juvenile Delinquency, Policing, Prosecution & Courts, Corrections and Specific Forms of Deviance & Prevention" (Meško, 2004: 537). Another very important publication on crime prevention is the textbook: *The Introduction to Crime Prevention* (Meško, 2002). Prepared especially for students and those who require some basic knowledge of crime prevention, this textbook deals with theoretical and empirical accomplishments in crime prevention in Western countries and Slovenia in the last decade. The main purpose of this textbook is to offer the reader a basic insight into crime prevention activities and efforts for better and safer communities. The reader should gain skills for critical thinking on many programmes, initiatives and ideas to reduce crime. The textbook has been accepted as obligatory reading material for students in several courses, which - among other topics - also deal with crime prevention.

Ideas on crime prevention have been changing in the last decade and been a part of a professional and political rhetoric. In addition to state responses to crime and the institutionalisation of crime control and crime prevention, non-governmental organisations have taken over preventative as well as educational/training activities (Meško, 2007).

Training in crime prevention has a quite long history in Slovenia, especially in the field of social and developmental crime prevention. There is no high school with a curriculum on crime prevention. Crime prevention as an undergraduate and postgraduate subject is, however, taught at the Faculty of Education (Social Pedagogy), the Faculty of Social Work (both University of Ljubljana) and at the Faculty of Criminal Justice and Security (University of Maribor). Since 1991, situational crime prevention has also been a part of the training, especially at the Faculty of Criminal Justice and Security (Meško, 2007). Therefore, we will focus only on crime prevention related to subjects taught at undergraduate and postgraduate levels of education at the Faculty of Criminal Justice and Security.

3. Study Programmes Related to Crime Prevention at the Faculty of Criminal Justice and Security

The Faculty of Criminal Justice and Security (FCJS) is the university-level research and study institution in the field of criminal justice studies, working to develop knowledge and offering new internationally comparable undergraduate and postgraduate programmes. The new educational programmes are adapted to the standards of the single 'European Higher Education Area' set out in the Bologna Declaration. One attempts to keep their contents up to date with the fast development of criminal justice and security knowledge and trends in »the relevant disciplines in Europe and around the world« (http://www.fvv.uni-mb.si).

The formation of our programmes has been well considered and before finalizing the study programmes, some programmes at West-European and American universities have been used for comparison. We took programmes of criminology and criminal justice into consideration that are taught at the University of Cambridge (Institute of Criminology), University of Leicester (Department of Criminology), University of Portsmouth (Institute of Criminal Justice Studies), Ruhr-Universität Bochum (Lehrstuhl für Kriminologie), University of Cincinnati (Criminal Justice graduate programmes), Florida State University, College of Criminology and Criminal Justice, Police Academy in Zagreb (Croatia), Hochschule für Polizei in Villingen-Schwenningen, Fachhochschule für Polizei Sachsen in Rothenburg and City University of New York (John Jay College of Criminal Justice). However, the comparison was not the only important part when forming new and adapting old programmes. A very important aspect that needed to be considered as well was the Slovenian cultural environment and its background. The aim was to design programmes that have the potential to make new contributions to the body of international knowledge in the mentioned field. Nevertheless, the mission of the Faculty of Criminal Justice and Security is to contribute to the field of criminal justice studies and security, which is based on the traditional vocational disciplines of Law, Sociology, Psychology, Political Science, Criminology, and Organisational Science, to share knowledge from this field with students and other users and to promote its application in everyday life where the important part is focused on crime prevention (http://www.fvv.uni-mb.si).

At the Faculty of Criminal Justice and Security, the "old" pre-Bologna declaration programmes consisted of several undergraduate programmes related to crime prevention, such as Theory of Social Control, Criminology, Victimology, Penology and Crime Prevention. The latter provides students with knowledge on crime prevention theories and policies of crime repression. The students learn which actions are advisable to take in dangerous, threatening situations. During the lessons, students get familiar with criminogenic and victimogenic circumstances that stimulate deviant behaviour of an individual or a group. Students gain knowledge of measures that can be used to act against potential delinquents. In addition to those mentioned classes, there are courses that are also somehow related to crime prevention: Theory of Policing, Criminal Investigation, and Analysis of Crime (within the topic of Research Methods). One of the "old" pre-Bologna declaration programmes was also a specialisation programme (graduate studies) consisting of a course 'Crime Prevention and Victimology'. This course focused on crime prevention in general but also on the prevention of secondary victimisation" (Meško, 2007). However, preventive actions are also a very important part of new study programmes, which follow the recommendations of the Bologna declaration; therefore they consist of subjects related to crime prevention and the provision of safety/security (Meško, 2007).

At the Faculty of Criminal Justice and Security there are four new study programmes that are available to students: two undergraduate and two postgraduate study programmes. A three – year undergraduate vocational study programme and a three – year undergraduate professionally oriented study programme consist of the following compulsory and optional subjects (see Figure 1 and Figure 2):

Figure 1: Undergraduate Vocational Study Programme

Diploma in Security and Police Work			
1st Year (60 ECTS)	**2nd Year (60 ECTS)**	**3rd Year (60 ECTS)**	
Core Subjects	Core Subjects	Optional Courses (1/5 = 18 ECTS)	Optional Subjects (3/21 = 18 ECTS)
Psychology (7 ECTS)	Criminal Law System of the Republic of Slovenia (7 ECTS)	*1. Security in Community*	Assessment of Security in Community (6 ECTS)
Basics of Sociology for Criminal Justice Professionals (6 ECTS)	Criminal Investigation (9 ECTS)	Assessment of Security in Community (6 ECTS)	Basic Concepts of Information Security (6 ECTS)
Criminology (8 ECTS)	Management and Organizational Behaviour (9 ECTS)	Introduction to Environmental Crime (6 ECTS)	Company Security System (6 ECTS)
Basics of Business Economics (6 ECTS)	Criminal Procedure in the Republic of Slovenia (7 ECTS)	Law Enforcement Powers of the Police and other State Agencies (6 ECTS)	Economic Crime (6 ECTS)
Introduction to Law Including Basic Principles of State Organization (8 ECTS)	International Security Cooperation (6 ECTS)	*2. Criminal Investigation*	Evaluation and Analysis and Intelligence and Security Services (6 ECTS)
National Security System (8 ECTS)	Methodology with Elements of Statistics (6 ECTS)	Organised Crime (6 ECTS)	Fundamental of Kinesiology in Criminal Justice and Security (6 ECTS)
Informatics and Computer Systems (6 ECTS)	Business Communication (6 ECTS)	Economic Crime (6 ECTS)	Human Rights and Law Enforcement Powers (6 ECTS)
Administrative Law and Public Administration (6 ECTS)	English/German-Slovene Criminal Justice and Security Terminology (5 ECTS)	Police and Forensic Psychology (6 ECTS)	Intelligence Services (6 ECTS)
Sport 1 (3 ECTS)	Sport 2 (3 ECTS)	*3. Private Security*	Introduction to Policing (6 ECTS)
Professional Skills (2 ECTS)	**Professional Skills (2 ECTS)**	Private Security and Private Investigation Activity (6 ECTS)	Law Enforcement Powers of the Police and Other State Agencies (6 ECTS)

Company Security System (6 ECTS)	Operational Collection of Intelligence and Security Information (6 ECTS)
Technical Security Systems (6 ECTS)	Organised Crime (6 ECTS)
4. Intelligence Security Services	Police and Forensic Psychology (6 ECTS)
Intelligence Services (6 ECTS)	Police Procedures (6 ECTS)
Operational Collection of Intelligence and Security Information (6 ECTS)	Police Work and Organization (6 ECTS)
Evaluation and Analysis and Intelligence and Security Services (6 ECTS)	Private Security and Private Investigation Activity (6 ECTS)
5. Operative Police Activities	Private Security Management (6 ECTS)
Introduction to Policing (6 ECTS)	Technical Security Systems (6 ECTS)
Police Work and Organization (6 ECTS)	Terrorism and Intelligence Activities (6 ECTS)
Human Rights and Law Enforcement Powers (6 ECTS)	The Introduction to Environmental Crime (6 ECTS)
Professional Skills (12 ECTS)	Traffic Delinquency Investigation and Prevention (6 ECTS)
Diploma Thesis (12 ECTS)	

Figure 2: Undergraduate BA Study Programme

Bachelor of Arts (BA) in Criminal Justice and Security			
1st Year (60 ECTS)	**2nd Year (60 ECTS)**	**3rd Year (60 ECTS)**	
Core Subjects	Core Subjects	Core Subject	Optional Courses (1/3 = 18 ECTS)
Theory of Social Control (6 ECTS)	Public Administration (6 ECTS)	Group Dynamics and Teamwork (6 ECTS)	*1. Public Security*
Ethics and Human Rights (6 ECTS)	Human Resource Management (6 ECTS)	Optional Subjects (4/9 = 24 ECTS)	Law Enforcement Powers in Criminal Investigation (6 ECTS)
Methodology of Social Research and Statistics (7 ECTS)	Criminal Law (7 ECTS)	Administrative Law and Administrative Legal Procedures (6 ECTS)	Strategy of Criminal Investigation (6 ECTS)
Basics of Information and Computer Systems (6 ECTS)	Criminal Procedure Law (6 ECTS)	Basic Course of Forensic Sciences (6 ECTS)	Theories of Policing (6 ECTS)
Jurisprudence with Constitutional Law (7 ECTS)	Criminal Investigation (8 ECTS)	Basics of Information Security (6 ECTS)	*2. Private and Business Security*
Psychology in Criminal Justice (7 ECTS)	Criminology (8 ECTS)	Interpersonal Communication (6 ECTS)	Technical Security Systems (6 ECTS)
Sociology (5 ECTS)	International Security Integrations (6 ECTS)	Investigative and Forensic Psychology (6 ECTS)	Private Security (6 ECTS)
Sport with Basics of Kinesiology (5 ECTS)	Organizational Behaviour (7 ECTS)	Management of Police Organizations (6 ECTS)	Business Security Systems and Security Markets (6 ECTS)
Basics of Economics (5 ECTS)	English or German Terminology and Written Discourse in Criminal Justice and Security (6 ECTS)	Methodology of Criminal Investigation (6 ECTS)	*3. Intelligence Analytical*
Security System (6 ECTS)		Misdemeanour Law (6 ECTS)	Intelligence and Security Systems (6 ECTS)

Transnational Threats to Security (6 ECTS)	Operational Methods of Intelligence Collection (6 ECTS)
Diploma Thesis (12 ECTS)	Methods of Evaluation and Analysis in Intelligence and Security Services (6 ECTS)

A two–year postgraduate MA study programme consists of the following core subjects, modules and optional subjects (see Figure 3):

Figure 3: Postgraduate MA Study Programme

MA in Criminal Justice and Security Studies	
1st Year (60 ECTS)	**2nd Year (60 ECTS)**
Core Subjects	**Core Subjects**
Constitutional Criminal Procedure (15 ECTS)	Critical Thinking and Problem-Solving (10 ECTS)
Elements of Crime Control Policy – Crime, Crime Prevention and Provision of Safety (15 ECTS)	Methodology of Social Research and Applied Multivariate Statistics (10 ECTS)
Optional Subjects (6/16 = 30 ECTS)	**Modules** (1/5 = 20 ECTS)
Advanced Topics in Violence and Violent Crime (5 ECTS)	*1. Policing*
Applied and Integrative Studies in CJ & Security (5 ECTS)	Strategic Management in Criminal Justice and Security Organizations (10 ECTS)
Business Intelligence (5 ECTS)	Comparison of Contemporary Policing Approaches (10 ECTS)
Corporate Safety and Security Culture and Business Organization (5 ECTS)	*2. Criminal Investigation*
Detection of Selected Forms of Transnational Crime (5 ECTS)	Criminal Investigation as a Gnoseological Process (10 ECTS)
Deviance at the Workplace (5 ECTS)	Crime Investigation Strategy of Crime Reduction (10 ECTS)

Drugs and Crime (5 ECTS)	**3. Applied Criminology**
Forensic Sciences (5 ECTS)	Sociological and Philosophical Aspects in Criminology (10 ECTS)
Insurance Industry and Security (5 ECTS)	Penal Policy and Penology (10 ECTS)
Management of Security Processes (5 ECTS)	**4. Intelligence and Security Activity**
Operative Police Management (5 ECTS)	Intelligence and Security Activity (10 ECTS)
Oversight of Intelligence and Security Systems (5 ECTS)	Psychosocial Aspects of Intelligence and Security Activity (10 ECTS)
Profiling in Criminal Investigation (5 ECTS)	**5. Business Security**
Selected Issues in Victimology (5 ECTS)	Industrial, Economic and Business Security (10 ECTS)
Systemic Aspects of the Protection of Secret Data (5 ECTS)	Private Security Industry (10 ECTS)
The Law of Evidence (5 ECTS)	**6. Peace Process and Humanitarian Law**
	Humanitarian Interventions and Peacekeeping Missions (10 ECTS)
	European and International Treaty Based Criminal Law (10 ECTS)
	MA Thesis Defence (20 ECTS)

The structure of a three–year PhD study programme in Criminal Justice and Security is presented in Figure 4:

Figure 4: Postgraduate PhD Study Programme

PhD Programme in Criminal Justice and Security Studies		
1st Year (60 ECTS)	**2nd Year (60 ECTS)**	**3rd Year (60 ECTS)**
Core Subjects	**Modules** (1/3 =30 ECTS)	Final Seminar (20 ECTS)
Theoretical Fundaments of National Security and Crime Control Policy (15 ECTS)	*1. Policing and Criminal Investigation*	**PhD Thesis Defence** (40 ECTS)
Behaviour, Leadership and Management in Criminal Justice and Security Organizations (15 ECTS)	Planning and Organization of Criminal Investigation (10 ECTS)	
Scientific Research of Security Phenomena (15 ECTS)	Policing in Contemporary Societies and Police Law (10 ECTS)	
Seminar (15 ECTS)	Criminal Investigative Aspects of Responses on Contemporary Forms of Criminality (10 ECTS)	
	2. Criminology	
	Comparative Criminology (10 ECTS)	
	Social Control in Post-Modern Society (10 ECTS)	
	European and International Treaty Based Criminal Law (10 ECTS)	
	3. Business Security	
	Intelligence and Security Activity and Oversight of Intelligence and Security Services (10 ECTS)	
	Theoretical and Systemic Aspects of Non-State Security and Security in Business Processes (10 ECTS)	

Social-Psychological Aspects of Intelligence and Security Activity (10 ECTS)

Individual Research (30 ECTS)

The above figures represent the complete structures of the study programmes. In addition, the courses related to crime prevention and the provision of safety will be discussed in more details (All the details of the FCJS study programmes can be found (in Slovenian) on the website of the University of Maribor (http://www.uni-mb.si)):

3.1 The Undergraduate Vocational Study Programme

Students gain basics of crime prevention theory in the compulsory subject Criminology. The course International Security Cooperation is designed to familiarize students with the role of international organisations, political and security organisations and international initiatives in the field of prevention and combating different forms of threats to the international community. Students learn about the EU security policy-making process, measures and organisations of the international community for the prevention of threats to security. The course is designed to provide understanding and application of theoretical and practical knowledge about the organisation and functioning of the EU and international security cooperation in combating international crime and other forms of threats to security. The course Organised Crime is, therefore, designed to provide an understanding and interpretation of organized crime groups and their activities, and to apply this knowledge to the domestic environment. Students gain the knowledge to compare different problems and learn to evaluate positive and negative effects. During the lessons, students also learn that the role of prevention is highly important in fighting organized crime; especially the media and NGOs can be a very valued element in preventive activities. They are in particular expected to play a role in helping the victims.

The problem of information security is taken into consideration in the course: Basic Concepts of Information Security. The course is designed to provide an overview of information security. Students are introduced to basic concepts of information security. Different information on security threats is presented in such a way that the knowledge about details of information technology is not essential. Students gain an understanding of the complexity and extreme dynamics of the field. They will acquire the capability to improve the status of information security in the company, and become aware of the importance of an information security policy. After this course, they will acquire knowledge about necessary actions in the case of information security breaches.

The course The Introduction to Environmental Crime is also one of the optional subjects in the third year of the undergraduate Vocational Study Programme. During the lessons, students learn the role and function of the police in connection with environmental accidents and pollution. They are introduced to the consequences of pollution for the ecosystem and the role of police work in the prevention and investigation of environmental crime. The course Assessment of Security in the Community discusses principles and procedures related to the assessment of security.

The details of the Slovenian national security system are discussed in the course National Security System, where students acquire knowledge and an understanding of multidimensional phenomena of security as a precondition for successful physical, spiritual and material development of individuals, groups, society and the state. They recognise basic elements of the national security system in a modern society and state, and basic organisational, structural and functional forms of security on the individual, national and international level.

The course Company Security Systems qualifies students to design security solutions. In the course Technical Security Systems students acquire knowledge of basic principles of technical security. The new technical and organisational trends in theft, burglary, robbery, fire, and explosion prevention will be presented. Furthermore, the course Private Security Management introduces students to the basics of private security and private security management. In the course Private Security and Private Investigative Activity students get knowledge of basic concepts of private security and private investigative activity. They gain insight into informal (non-state) mechanisms and instruments of security and learn about the national security elements of private security and private investigative activity. They also learn about the specifics of private security in comparison to state security agencies. In the courses Introduction to Policing, Police Work and Organization, Law Enforcement Powers of the Police and Other State Agencies, and Human Rights and Law Enforcement Powers, students gain more knowledge about state security agencies and their obligations and tasks.

After completing the undergraduate vocational study programme, students are able to use scientific methods for solving professional and work problems. The students are qualified especially for practical work (http://www.fvv.uni-mb.si).

3.2 Undergraduate BA Study Programme

The basics of crime prevention theory are taught in the course Criminology. The objective of the course Theory of Social Control is to provide students with basic knowledge to understand the role of social control in contemporary society and learn about control agencies in Slovenia and Europe. The course introduces students to major theoretical and practical concepts of social control in society. Through case studies and exercises, the course enables students to develop skills for understanding a variety of forms of social control.

In the course International Security Integrations students will become familiar with the OSCE and with other organizations responsible for security in Europe, including major non-governmental human rights organizations, police, judicial, and other cooperations in the prevention and repression of transnational crime, with security risks and their prevention.

Causes and forms of modern transnational threats are discussed in the course Transnational Threats to Security, where students acquire knowledge about modern threats and obtain skills enabling them to analyse global security threats. Using various sources and considering the global developments, students analyse trends in threats and try to apply the acquired knowledge to the situation in Slovenia. Students learn about the significance of cooperation between agencies that contribute to an overall consideration of security threats.

When searching for the best solutions in crime prevention, the knowledge acquired in Strategy of Criminal Investigation could be very helpful. In this course students learn how to understand the importance of the formation of strategies of criminal investigation for efficient crime control. They acquire skills for the evaluation of different factors in connection with the use of advantages and disadvantages and the capability of forecasting the consequences of the implementation of new strategies and the neutralisation of non-desired objectives. The course enables students to prepare strategic documents in the field of crime control. Details of the Slovene national security system are discussed in the course Security System. The course enables students to recognize and understand a system of national security in the modern state (strategy, functioning of the modern security system). There is some emphasis on governance, guidance, and the functioning of the subjects of the national security system as well as on control over it. Students will be taught to understand the meaning and the content of doctrines and legal acts in relation to the security system.

The discussions about the methods of how society should provide for its own safety regarding the most frequently committed offences, such as property and violent crimes are (among others) debated in the optional course Methodology of Criminal Investigation.

The problem of information security is also taken into consideration in the undergraduate professionally oriented study programme. In the course Basics of Information Security students are introduced to basic concepts of information security. The course is designed to provide an overview of the field of information security. Different information on security threats is presented in such a way that knowledge about details of information technology is not essential. Students gain an understanding of the complexity and extreme dynamics of the field. They will acquire the competence to improve the status of information security in the company, and learn to be aware of the importance of an information security policy. After the course, they will acquire the knowledge of necessary actions in the case of information security breaches.

In the course Business Security Systems and Security Markets students get familiar with the legislation in individual fields of security. The course presents a methodology and process of assessment and control of vulnerability and security risks in businesses. After attending these lessons, students are qualified for the preparation of projects, internal documents, plans and for giving instruction to security and protection. The course Technical Security Systems imparts knowledge of the basic principles of technical security and how to provide it. New technical and organisational trends in theft, burglary, robbery, fire, and explosion prevention will be presented. The course Private Security imparts basic knowledge of private security and private investigative activities, and students gain insight into the development of a system of legal regulation of private security. They will acquire knowledge about private security activities as a part of national security. After taking the course, students should be able to critically evaluate the interference of non-state actors in the field of security of individuals, groups and society, and to analyse the relations and conflicts between state and non-state security organizations.

Students gain more knowledge of state security organizations and their obligations and tasks in the courses Theories of Policing and Management of Police Organizations, Law Enforcement Powers in Criminal Investigations and Ethics and Human Rights. In addition to the courses indicated above, Psychology in Criminal Justice is also somehow related to crime prevention, especially in the part of psychiatry in criminal justice.

After completing the undergraduate professionally oriented study programme, students are able to understand, conduct and manage more complex processes of provision of (state) safety. The knowledge of critical thinking they gain enables them to perform professional tasks independently and carry out analytical, creative and innovative problem-solving tasks (http://www.fvv.uni-mb.si).

Crime prevention, however, is not only the topic of undergraduate courses. In postgraduate MA and PhD study programmes, there are several courses related to crime prevention.

3.3 Postgraduate MA study programme
Developing responses to crime and deviance is one of the elementary tasks in the domain of criminal policy. The course Elements of Crime Control Policy - Crime, Crime Prevention and Provision of Safety enables students to identify and understand the need for an organised and planned provision of safety, security and crime prevention and teaches them to apply the appropriate measures to certain social contexts.

The course Advanced Topics in Violence and Violent Crime provides students with in-depth knowledge, understanding and utilization of relevant theoretical issues, concepts and strategies within the framework of violence in interpersonal relations. It offers valuable knowledge to policy-makers, researchers, practitioners, advocates and volunteers involved in violence prevention. The main topics also related to crime prevention are: youth violence, child abuse and neglect by parents and other caregivers, violence by intimate partners, sexual violence, and abuse of the elderly.

Furthermore, the course Drugs and Crime introduces students to major theoretical and practical concepts, which explain the phenomenon of the correlation of drugs and crime as well as specific methods for their understanding and conceptualisation. Through case studies and exercises, the course enables students to develop skills for understanding problems related to drug addiction and crime prevention. Students also get familiar with the National Programme of Drug-Related Problems 2004-2009 (National Programme against Drug Abuse 2004–2009) (National Gazette, 28/2004) and problems in connection with reducing drug–related crimes.

Students can acquire more advanced knowledge about transnational crime in the postgraduate course Detection of Selected Forms of Transnational Crime. During their studies they will become familiar with the role of crime prevention (especially with the role of the media, NGOs etc.), the role of international institutions in preventing transnational crime and activities of criminal groups, international trends in and techniques to fight against transnational crime, problems of cooperation, and the role of Slovenia in the prevention of transnational crime.

The course Selected Issues in Victimology enables students to understand the position of a victim in criminal procedure as well as social and individual consequences of criminal victimization. Through the case studies and exercises, the course enables students to develop skills for the proper treatment of victims of crime.

Crime prevention takes an important place also in the Insurance Industry and Security class. In this course students learn about the theoretical and practical aspects of insurance industry as a social mechanism for the security of individuals and social groups in modern society.

The course is designed to provide the knowledge necessary for understanding the role and social usefulness of the insurance industry as an important security mechanism in a society at individual and common/social level, as well as insurance industry as an important economic activity. Students learn to distinguish different dimensions of security, circumstances and causes of threats and actual possibilities and forms of insurance against them offered by the insurance industry. Students also recognise fundamental forms of insurance and their meaning for individual and common/social security. Moreover, the theoretical and practical aspects of the insurance industry as a social mechanism for the security of individuals and social groups in modern society are discussed as well.

Crime prevention is more effective if its role and the crime itself are well understood. Therefore, the optional course Applied and Integrative Studies in CJ & Security discusses the increase in crime and its meaning to society. In this course, students learn about theoretical, integrative and practical dimensions of crime and details about the context and how to find practical solutions to reduce crime and delinquency. They should learn to understand the complexity of situations that cause crime, modern criminological trends, multidisciplinarity, and the need for contextualisation in the use of theory in explaining crime and criminality.

Through case studies and exercises, the course enables students to develop skills for solving problems related to understanding of crime and criminality. The course introduces students to major theoretical and practical concepts explaining crime and criminality as well as specific methods for their understanding and conceptualisation. Some topics are also dedicated to crime prevention and its importance in the fight against crime.

Students can gain advanced knowledge on private security in the course Corporate Safety and Security Culture and Business Organization, which enables students to develop the business process security model that is based on ethical and development principles. In the second year of their MA study programme students can select the module *Private and Business Security,* where crime prevention in the private sector is discussed in more detail. The course Industrial, Economic and Business Security (second year of the MA study programme) is designed to provide knowledge and research skills necessary for understanding the role and functions of security mechanisms in industry and economy. Students are qualified for an innovative participation in carrying out security analyses, security studies and security discussions and are able to offer security consulting to owners and managers. The course is designed to provide students with the knowledge and skills necessary for independent and team-based problem solving, project management, carrying out security analyses, planning security improvements (upgrades), and security market management. Another course in the module *Private and Business Security* is Private Security Industry. The topics with a connection to crime prevention are especially civilian self-protection, civil initiative, interest groups and other associations as forms of security self-organisation of civil society; and company security systems, the security market, the quality of the private security industry, private security management, control over private security and other specifics of the private security industry.

The course Crime Investigation Strategy of Crime Reduction discusses concerns of crime prevention and crime-reducing strategies. Students will become familiar with strategic planning in crime investigation as part of the problem-solving process and with the analysis of different strategies for crime control with respect to theoretical tools of crime investigation strategy. After the lessons students are trained to prepare different strategic documents in the field of crime control.

Furthermore, the optional course Comparison of Contemporary Policing Approaches deals with community policing (in Slovenia, Europe and other countries), maintaining order in communities, and crime prevention and local safety in communities.
Furthermore, students can gain more advanced knowledge of crime prevention in the MA module *Applied Criminology*. The subjects Sociological and Philosophical Aspects in Criminology and Penal Policy and Penology disclose some modern aspects of criminology and penology that are important for a better placement of crime prevention in society.

However, familiarity with police work is also fundamental for understanding the special features of repressive and preventive activities of the police. Therefore, the students can attend the course Operative Police Management that discusses policing.

The goal of the MA study programme is to educate the specialists of criminal justice and security. After completing this programme, students are able to understand the trends in the field of social control, criminal justice and security. They gain advanced knowledge of the sociological, psychological, philosophical, economic, behavioural, historic and political aspects of crime, deviance and the criminal justice system. Nevertheless, students also gain more advanced knowledge in the field of crime prevention and reduction of criminal offences (http://www.fvv.uni-mb.si).

3.4 Postgraduate PhD study programme

The course Social Control in Post-Modern Society discusses different forms of social control in post-modern society, contemporary security policies in Western society, and the meaning of institutionalized and non-institutionalized social control and its influences on society. The outcome of this course should be an understanding of the main characteristics of pro-active and re-active mechanisms of social control in post-modern capitalism.

 Another optional subject, where students gain very important information for understanding crime and its dimensions, is Comparative Criminology. In this course students get an insight into important aspects of comparative criminology and criminal justice and learn about cultural, political and economic factors having an impact on the understanding of crime, law enforcement and responses to crime and deviance.

Students gain a complex insight into criminal policy in the course Theoretical Fundaments of National Security and Crime Control Policy. Students learn about Security Policy in contemporary, post-modern society; contents and specificity of the national security policy; processes of making and implementing such policies – policy process; phases of the policy process; formal and informal actors and factors of the creation of security policy; components of security policy; crime control and prevention policy; crime control and repression; crime prevention; institutional coordination (vertical/horizontal); factors of crime policy changes (e.g. cascade events); accountability issues; measurement of the effects of crime control and prevention policy; and about crime and social control, where the new interdisciplinary approaches to crime reduction and modes of social control are explained. The course introduces students to major theoretical and practical concepts of safety/security policies and crime control. During these lessons, students learn about processes of the formation of security and crime policies, current security policies of European countries, national crime policies of European countries, and about mechanisms for providing safety and security and for the reduction of crime. Through case studies and exercises, the course enables students to develop skills for understanding national and international security and safety policies as well as national and international crime control policies, strategies and practices.

The course Criminal Investigative Aspects of Responses on Contemporary Forms of Criminality introduces students to the latest theoretical and practical concepts of curbing current forms of criminality. Through case studies and exercises, the course enables students to develop skills for understanding contemporary forms of criminality and analyse suitable measures in the EU framework for curbing criminality.

Furthermore, students gain more progressive knowledge on the private security industry in the course Theoretical and Systemic Aspects of Non-State Security and Security in Business Processes (second year of PhD study programme). The course enables students to understand the theoretical and systemic aspects of non-state security with emphasis on private security as well as the development of non-state security. Students gain advanced knowledge of state security and its role in preventive work in the course Policing in Contemporary Societies and Police Law.

The goal of the PhD study programme is to educate experts of criminal justice and security. After completing this programme, the students are able to understand recent events in the world related to security issues. They understand the complexity of trends of social control and criminal justice and security. They gain expert knowledge of sociological, psychological, philosophical, economic, behavioural, historic and political aspects of crime, deviance and the criminal justice system. Furthermore, they learn to do research work in the field of criminal justice and criminal procedure, and to introduce improvements into police work, prosecution work and into the work of prison facilities. In the PhD study programme, students also gain expert knowledge in the field of crime prevention and reduction of criminal offences (http://www.fvv.uni-mb.si).

Most of the presented courses consist of lectures, seminars, discussions, case studies, individual and group projects, and individual consultations with the respective professor. During the studies (in all the available study programmes), students need to study some articles in professional journals (such as Bučar-Ručman and Meško, 2006) and some textbooks that are accepted as obligatory student material in several classes, which - among other topics - also deal with crime prevention (Meško, 2006; Dvoršek and Selinšek, 2004; Dobovšek, 1997; Bučar-Ručman, 2004; Kanduč, 2005; Meško, 2002; Meško, 2007a; Anžič, Meško and Plazar, 2004; Meško, 2004; Meško and Dobovšek, 2007).

4. Concluding Remarks

Crime prevention could be interpreted as a mosaic, consisting of different types of knowledge. This knowledge should be used in searching for better and more efficient solutions to reduce crime. The most important element influencing this is the educational system. It gives students the knowledge and skills for individual work, critical thinking and goal-oriented planning.

The Faculty of Criminal Justice and Security therefore offers four new study programmes on criminal justice and security, where crime prevention plays an important role. The programmes follow the recommendations of the Bologna declaration and provide courses in criminal justice and security studies to undergraduate and postgraduate students. We are trying to keep the content of the study programmes up to date with the fast development of criminal justice and security knowledge and the trends in »the relevant disciplines in Europe and around the world«. Recent changes in Slovenia "call for a mixed model of accountable state and local professionals, as well as the contribution of civil society". The main goal of new programmes is to make a new contribution to the body of international knowledge of criminal justice and security, where crime prevention plays an important role. Therefore, the "ambitiously created study programmes in criminal justice and security studies reflect the needs of safety/security specialists in state/local government institutions, both in civil society and in NGOs dealing with crime and security problems (Meško, Bučar-Ručman, Tominc, and Maver, 2007: 236-237).

References

Anžič, A., Meško, G., Plazar, J. (Eds.). (2004). *Mladoletniško nasilje – zbornik razprav (Youth Violence – Collection of Essays)*. Ljubljana: Ministrstvo za notranje zadeve, Policija.

Bučar-Ručman, A. (2004). *Nasilje in mladi (Violence and the Youth)*. Ljubljana: Klub mladinski kulturni center Novo mesto.

Bučar Ručman, A., Meško, G. (2006). Presentation of Police Activities in the Mass Media. *Journal of Criminal Justice and Security*, 8/3-4, str. 223-234.

Dobovšek, B. (1997). *Organizirani criminal (Organised Crime)*. Ljubljana: Unigraf.

Dvoršek, A. (2004). Nekateri (kriminalistično) strateški vidiki preprečevanja kriminalitete. In Meško, G. (Ed.), *Preprečevanje kriminalitete – teorija, praksa in dileme (Crime Prevention – Theory, Practice and Dilemmas)*. Ljubljana: Inštitut za kriminologijo pri Pravni fakulteti v Ljubljani, pp. 260-270.

Dvoršek, A., Selinšek, L. (2004). *Goljufije v zavarovalništvu (Frauds in the Insurance Industry)*. Maribor: Univerza v Mariboru, Fakulteta za varnostne vede in Pravna fakulteta.

Frangež, D. (2007). Strategija omejevanja vlomov (v objekte) v Sloveniji (*Strategy of Burglary Prevention in Slovenia*). In Lobnikar, B. (Ed.), *Slovenski dnevi varstvoslovja*. Ljubljana: Univerza v Mariboru, Fakulteta za varnostne vede, str. 1-12.

Kanduč, Z. (2004). Postmoderno stanje in družbeno nadzorstvo (*Postmodern State of Social Control*). *Revija za kriminalistiko in kriminologijo*, 55/1, str. 3-21.

Kanduč, Z. (ur.). (2005). *Kriminaliteta, družbeno nadzorstvo in postmodernizacijski procesi (Crime, Social Control and Postmodern Processes)*. Ljubljana: Inštitut za kriminologijo pri Pravni fakulteti.

Meško, G. (2000). Pogledi na preprečevanje kriminalitete v poznomodernih družbah *(Aspects of Crime Prevention in Post-Modern Societies)*. In Pagon, M. (Ed.), *Slovenski dnevi varstvoslovja*. Ljubljana: Visoka policijsko-varnostna šola, str. 295-305.

Meško, G. (2002). *Osnove preprečevanja kriminalitete (Basics of Crime Prevention)*. Ljubljana: Univerza v Mariboru, Fakulteta za varnostne vede.

Meško, G. (2006). *Kriminologija (Criminology)*. Ljubljana: Univerza v Mariboru, Fakulteta za varnostne vede.

Meško, G. (2007). *Status Report of the Professional Training in Crime Prevention – Slovenia*. Presentation at the Beccaria partner meeting, professional training in crime prevention. Hanover, Germany, from 27th to 28th April.

Meško, G. (Ed.). (2004). *Preprečevanje kriminalitete - teorija, praksa in dileme (Crime prevention - Theory, Practice and Dilemmas)*. Ljubljana: Inštutut za kriminologijo pri Pravni fakulteti v Ljubljani.

Meško, G. (Ed.). (2007a). *Izbrana poglavja iz viktimologije I. – mala čitanka za varstvoslovce (Selected Topics on Victimology)*. Ljubljana: Univerza v Mariboru, Fakulteta za varnostne vede.

Meško, G., Bučar-Ručman, A., Tominc, B., Maver, D. (2007). Challenges of Local Safety in Slovenia: on the Path of Good Will, Responsible Citizenry and Managerialism. In Meško, G., Dobovšek, B. (Eds.), *Policing in Emerging Democracies – Critical Reflections*. Ljubljana: Univerza v Mariboru, Fakulteta za varnostne vede, str. 209-242.

Meško, G., Dobovšek, B. (Eds.). (2007). *Policing in Emerging Democracies – Critical Reflections*. Ljubljana: Univerza v Mariboru, Fakulteta za varnostne vede.

Meško, G., Vogrinec, M. (2003). Pojmovanje preprečevanja kriminalitete in zagotavljanja varnosti v lokalni skupnosti *(Understanding of Crime Prevention and Provision of Safety in a Local Community)*. In Pagon, M. (Ed.), *Slovenski dnevi varstvoslovja*. Ljubljana: Visoka policijsko-varnostna šola, str. 1-8.

Pečar, J. (1988). *Formalno nadzorstvo: kriminološki in kriminalnopolitični pogledi (The Informal Social Control)*. Ljubljana: Delavska enotnost.

Pečar, J. (1991). *Neformalno nadzorstvo: kriminološki in sociološki pogledi (The Formal Social Control)*. Radovljica: Didakta.

Pečar, J. (1992). *Institucionalizirano nedržavno družbeno nadzorstvo: kriminološki, kriminalnopolitični in sociološki pogledi (The Institutionalized Informal Social Control)*. Radovljica: Didakta.

Pečar, J. (2002). Preprečevanje kriminalitete in policija *(Crime Prevention and Police)*. In Pagon, M. (Ed.), *Slovenski dnevi varstvoslovja*. Ljubljana: Visoka policijsko-varnostna šola, str. 1-12.

Rejc Buhovac, A., Savič, N., Krševan, E., Pevcin, P., Meško, G. (2007). *Analiza vzrokov odškodninskih zahtevkov pri uporabi policijskih prisilnih sredstev in ukrepi za njihovo odpravo : končno poročilo raziskovalnega projekta v okviru CRP 2001-2006 (An Analysis of the Reasons for Damage Claims for the Police (Ab)Use of Force and Measures for Eliminating Them: Summary of Key Findings of the Project within the Target-oriented Research Programme "Slovenian Competitiveness 2001-2006")*. Ljubljana: Ekonomska fakulteta.

National programme against drug abuse 2004-2009. Official Gazette, Republic of Slovenia, 28/2004.

The National crime prevention and Crime Control Strategy of the Republic of Slovenia. Official Gazette, Republic of Slovenia, 40/2007.

The Mid–term Plan of Police Work for period 2003-2007. Accessed at http://www.policija.si on July 25, 2007.

Faculty of Criminal Justice and Security. Accessed at http://www.fvv.uni-mb.si on July 25, 2007.

The Slovenian Police. Accessed at http://www.policija.si on July 25, 2007.

Charlotte B. Vincent

Status Report Denmark - Status of Programmes/Continuing Education in the Field of Crime Prevention

Introduction

The work of crime prevention is initiated and conducted in a social arena that embraces numerous values, attitudes, political goals as well as several professions with different professional approaches (social workers, psychologists, teachers, and police). This arena also contains specific locally and institutionally defined frameworks for courses of action.

This is the challenge for crime prevention work and the reality in which it unfolds in line with other social work. A discussion of programmes/continuing education in the field of crime prevention presents some rather complex and special challenges. Part of the difficulty lies in limiting, defining and creating consensus on the nature of crime prevention.[4]

The various actors and professional stakeholders in the field often develop their own perception of crime prevention based on their specific professional backgrounds. This is shown, for example, in the many different crime prevention projects that are often based on widely varying perceptions of prevention, theories and methods.

Numerous professionals in the social arena have quite different approaches to crime prevention, differences that are reflected in their choice of specific measures and actions. These activities span from formal police work at street level to more general terror prevention, parole for offenders, private security services, self-protection of the individual in daily life, etc. One way to improve and develop these activities at both the individual and the institutional level is to improve people's ability to analyse and evaluate activities and actions, including the professional's own role in crime prevention.

Many training and education initiatives at various levels and to differing degrees are currently underway in Denmark. All of the initiatives I will be mentioning are continuing education courses aimed in one way or another at daily crime prevention practitioners, as well as full programmes such as the diploma programme in criminology and short courses in the field.

Denmark has approx. 30,000 people who are involved in crime prevention work in some way. Police officers, social workers, prison personnel, street workers, judges, educators, lawyers,

---

[4] The Danish Crime Prevention Council (DKR) always sets out its rationale before initiating crime prevention measures: humanitarian considerations, values, target groups, choice of method, basis for assessment/evaluation.

drug counsellors, private guards, journalists, SSP consultants[5], doctors and many other professional groups to some extent deal with crime prevention as part of their profession.

1. Diploma Programme in Criminology

The diploma programme is offered jointly by the Schools of Social Work in Aarhus and Odense and by the University of Copenhagen in cooperation with the Copenhagen College of Social Work.

The diploma programme in criminology provides a formal qualification or upgrade and is targeted primarily at people with approximately three years of higher education (corresponding to a bachelor's degree) from a School of Social Work, Police Academy, College of Education, College of Nursing or a similar institution.

Crime and crime prevention are popular subjects for research in Denmark and internationally, and a large body of knowledge exists on effectively preventing and combating crime.

However, it seems that currently these many different types of knowledge are far from being fully utilized. The various professional groups do not exchange experience to any great extent, and practitioners seldom make use of the research-based knowledge about impact and effectiveness.

This is where the Diploma Programme in Criminology would like to make a difference. The programme has two main aims: first to give participants solid methodical and technical tools enabling them to retrieve relevant information, evaluate scientific results, and most important of all, convert this knowledge into concrete action. The second programme aim is to promote cooperation and knowledge-sharing between the various professional groups who deal with crime.

The general aim of the programme is thus to expand each participant's *toolbox* by providing solid, relevant, research-based knowledge about key topical criminological issues. The two-year programme is designed so that participants can take courses alongside their full-time jobs. The programme combines compulsory and elective modules that give participants an understanding of criminology as a science targeted at the causes, spread and effects of crime, as well as teaching them about criminology theory and empiricism related to their own daily work.

---

[5] An interdisciplinary, cross-sector Danish institution known as SSP: formalized local cooperation between schools, social administration and the police.

In this process, all the participants will learn about the penal system of police, courts and prisons, various control methods and crime prevention work. Participants can also undertake more in-depth studies of the prison system, police efforts, victims of crime and several aspects of drugs and alcohol-related issues.

Structure of the Diploma Programme
The programme is targeted at people whose work brings them in contact with crime. It provides a broad introduction to the background, systems and methods of criminology, and gives participants knowledge that can form the basis for more rational ways to combat and prevent crime.

The diploma programme in Criminology is based on a modular system: the full programme consists of six modules, of which modules 1, 2, 5 and 6 are compulsory. Modules 3 and 4 are electives to be chosen from those offered under the programme Diploma in Social Work, which includes a module on drugs and alcohol. The individual modules can also be taken as part of a more limited programme that does not lead to a diploma.

Module 1: Introduction to Criminology (compulsory)
This module is intended to lay a common foundation for the rest of the programme and thus contains an introduction to the other compulsory modules and electives.

A body of scientific theory is presented as a springboard to more in-depth treatment of the science of criminology. The most important theories on the nature of crime and how it arises are dealt with. Theories are presented in their own social and temporal context. Emphasis is placed on theories of European origin and of recent date.

Various methods for measuring the extent of crime are also presented. Light is shed on the possibilities and difficulties of using statistics as well as supplementary methods such as victim surveys and self-reporting. The meaning and extent of unreported figures in relation to various types of crime are included as an aid to understanding the difficulties of uncovering the true extent of crime. The most important authoritative sources of crime development statistics, which include a discussion of various levels of measurement in Denmark, are a major contribution to this end.

Finally, studies and ideas about the impact of crime in very different contexts, both societal (economic impact and impact on crime policy, for example) and personal (impact on the victim as well as the perpetrator) are presented.

Towards the end of the module, general guidance is provided on examination requirements for the programme and how to tackle written projects.

Competence Goals

After completing this module, participants will have mastered the most common causal explanations for crime and can express themselves independently and critically on the subject on a solid professional and objective basis. They can put the development of registered criminality in Denmark into perspective, explaining causal theories and crime policies in a firmly grounded, professional and objective way.

Module 2: The Penal System (compulsory)

After a general review of the progress of a criminal case from the time a report is made until sentencing, with emphasis on the division of labour between the police, the National Probation Service and the social authorities, the focus turns sharply to the response system. In the interests of the need for cross-sector cooperation in conjunction with penal response, various response options are reviewed, including the social, healthcare and penal systems relevant to various groups of people and types of crime. Participants are expected to contribute actively on the basis of their own experiences, for example, by discussing legitimate goals for the job such as result orientation, finances, ethics, confidentiality, etc.

Criminological and practical knowledge about the development, use and effect of various types of punishment are taken up throughout the module. Naturally, other forms of social control are also dealt with. This module paves the way for module 5.

Competence goals

After completing this module, participants will be able to explain in broad outline the penal process from the time a crime is reported until the perpetrator is sentenced. Participants will have gained insight into and an understanding of their own and other relevant professional groups' options and limitations in clearing up the case, sentencing, and the sanction phase. Participants will be able to explain key aspects of the choice of sanction relative to different groups of people and types of crime. Participants should also be familiar with the most significant features of the various forms of sanction and the extent to which they are applied.

Modules 3 and 4 (electives):
Police Research

The module presents a general review of the role and tasks of the police in the broad sense, now and in the past. International and Danish regulations, selected reading and selected studies of police work are included. Practical police work, including methods and their effectiveness in everyday situations and in crises will be described and discussed; for example, in the light of the development in registered crime and studies of the public's perception of security.

Competence goals

This module attempts to enhance the participants' knowledge of the content and effect of the key services provided by the police, as well as the set of rules on which police work is based. In the process, participants are expected to gain insight into the potential and limitations of cooperation between the police and other public authorities regarding selected types of tasks and groups of people. Finally, participants will gain insight into relevant methods of evaluating different types of police work, and they will also have ample opportunity to strengthen their own exercise of authority.

The choice of the project topic, method and theory is up to the individual participant. Participants will formulate the research issue in agreement with the teacher in charge before embarking on the project. Participants should be able to complete the project within the approx. 400 pages of the syllabus. The evaluation will emphasize whether the project achieved the competence goals for the module and whether it complied with the general requirements for documentation and use of sources and references.

Victims of Crime: Victimology, Sense of Justice and Witness Psychology
This module focuses on the victims of and witnesses to crime. Instruction covers key aspects of existing theories and empiricism about who is most often exposed to crime (and under what circumstances the risk is greatest) as well as practical and theoretical options for supporting victims, such as crisis centres, victim counselling, conflict councils etc. The victim of a crime often plays a key role as a witness in the formal penal process. The authorities' handling of this 'double role' needs to focus strongly on the awareness of professional considerations and ethics while ensuring that the requirements for evidence of guilt are met before the accused is sentenced. This problem complex is illuminated on the basis of well-known empirical evidence, literature, etc. about attitudes to punishment and the involvement of victims in the penal process.

Competence Goals
After completing this module, participants will have increased their understanding of the double role of the penal process: the obligation to find evidence of guilt and the weighty ethical consideration of preventing further victimization. Through studies and practical exercises, participants will also gain insight into various conflict solution models, as well as skills in dealing with difficult conflict situations.

Prison and Institution Research
This module deals primarily with prisons, but other types of institutions involved in the execution of a sentence are also considered. Instruction builds further on the general knowledge participants acquired about the penal system in module 2. Historical explanations of the origin of prisons and their design and use through the centuries will be reviewed. However, the instruction will mainly focus on how sentences are served in Danish prisons today, including the key rights and obligations of prisoners, current treatment and training options, other programmes, etc. Participants will be introduced to practical experience in how sentences are served in other countries, as well as UN and European minimum regulations for serving a sentence. Key sections of Danish legislation on the execution of a sentence, with detailed circulars, will be studied in the light of international regulations and knowledge of practice. The

course will also cover existing opportunities for alternative sentence serving and alternative types of punishment. We try to arrange a visit to a prison for interested participants.

Competence Goals

Participants will increase their understanding of why imprisonment is the predominant form of punishment in Denmark today, and what it really means: in other words, what daily life is like behind bars. By learning about international regulations and standards, participants will form their own view of the meaning of prisoners' rights, etc. based on knowledge (historical and international) of experience with treatment and other programmes.

Module 5: Crime Prevention (compulsory). Theories about the Causes of Crime and the Opportunities to Prevent it on Three Levels: Society, Group and Individual

This module builds directly on module 1 with regard to exploring various theoretical causal explanations for crime, and to some extent on module 2 and the penal system. Participants study the explanations for the causes of crime and the choices of response, with special emphasis on knowledge of effective prevention. We work with prevention on three levels: society, special target groups and the individual. Because we will be working with primary, secondary and tertiary prevention, this module will also raise a discussion on the effect of various types of initiatives. The opportunity to benefit from the experience of other countries will play a natural part in the discussion, and time will also be devoted to current Danish crime policy.

Competence Goals

After completing this module, participants will be aware of the basic concepts used in crime prevention theory and be familiar with important international experience with crime prevention on all three levels. They will be able to independently put their experience into perspective with regard to the Danish initiatives in word and practice.

Module 6: Final Project (compulsory)

The module starts by summarizing the content of the completed modules and putting it into perspective. An introduction to key scientific theories follows, including questions about scientific methods particularly relevant to criminal investigation. This is based in part on presentations from participants and leads directly to the final project preparation.

Before participants go their separate ways to work on their final projects, they will receive a general introduction on how to write a project description, research topic/issue, etc., and how to conduct small-scale scientific projects/studies.

The final project can be conducted individually or in small groups of up to three participants. Each participant/group must have its research topic/issue and project description approved by the responsible teacher before starting the project. Participants may receive limited project guidance underway. A written and oral evaluation of the diploma programme is made in conclusion.

Competence Goals

By carrying out the final project, participants must prove their ability to isolate a criminology problem and outline and carry through a plan to deal with it. In the process, participants must independently retrieve the relevant data and select the theories and literature relevant to the project. Finally, participants should be able to justify and put their project into perspective in relation to a relevant practice area.

Overview

Compulsory modules	Introduction to Criminology (9 ECTS)	History and methods of criminology Extent and development of criminology
	The Penal system, Social Control, Exercise of Authority and Ethics (9 ECTS)	Penal sanctions Exercise of authority in the penal system
	Crime Prevention (9 ECTS)	Theories about criminality and prevention Prevention in practice
Elective modules	Victims of Crime (9 ECTS)	Who becomes a victim and how can they best be supported? Witness psychology and practical ways to deal with witnesses
	Police Research (9 ECTS)	The role of the police in society What works in practical policing?
	Prison and Institution Research (9 ECTS)	The function of prisons Ideals and practice in working with prisoners
	Theoretical Perspectives in Social Work in the Area of Drugs and Alcohol (9ECTS)	Theoretical perspectives on drugs and alcohol
	Social Work Methods in the Area of Drugs and Alcohol (9ECTS)	Practical work in the area of drugs and alcohol
Compulsory final project	(15 ECTS)	A project connected to one or more modules is formulated.

2. A Diploma Programme in Social Education – with Special Emphasis on the Area Covered by SSP Employees and Consultants

The need to develop the competences of employees involved in SSP cooperation varies, depending on their tasks and level of responsibility.

The programme consists of three modules from the diploma programme in Social Education and one module from the diploma programme in Education plus two elective modules:

- Scientific theory and education
- Change processes and project management
- Socially disadvantaged groups
- Normality and deviation in modern society
- Counselling and supervision as a personal qualifying learning process *or* Conflict resolution
- Final project

Scientific Theory and Education; Scientific Theory in an SSP Perspective

This is often the introductory module for participants planning to take the full diploma programme, as the other modules build on this one. Participants can also take this module in parallel with or after other modules in the programme. The module presents the theories and research results significant to the work of SSP employees and consultants. Emphasis is also placed on acquiring skills in describing, evaluating and reflecting on the participant's own SSP work. The compulsory scientific theory module is essential to the identity and competency profile of the diploma programme.

Competences

The module Scientific Theory provides the following competences:

- broad basic knowledge of qualitative and quantitative theories and methods and their respective application and limitations;
- an introduction to the use of methods and research strategies in the social sciences and the associated considerations concerning research topics/issues, choice of method, planning, data collection and analysis;
- theoretical insight into and practical experience with planning, conducting and using interviews in connection with social science research topics/issues;
- theoretical insight into and practical experience with planning questionnaire surveys and designing questionnaires based on social science research topics/issues, as well as using and processing material in connection with specific projects;
- skills in the qualitative analysis of written interviews and other types of text.

Module 2: Change Processes and Project Management. The module is designed specifically for SSP employees and consultants and focuses on process management.

With change processes as the goal, participants work simultaneously with other modules in conjunction with their daily work. Theories from other modules and practical experience are incorporated and used directly or indirectly in the change process.

By managing new change processes, participants are expected to demonstrate that they can use and convert theory into practice in specific development work.

Participants individually select an area as their focus in terms of managing a development project. Theory relevant to development work will be taught throughout the duration of the module, and participants will have ongoing opportunities to share experiences with other participants.

The final project is expected to be related to the change process the participant has worked on throughout the diploma programme.

The curriculum includes the following:
- content;
- theories, methods and concepts about modernization and change processes;
- models and methods in project and development work;
- consultant and communication activities;
- communication theories;
- teaching and communication.

The goal is for participants:
• to acquire insight into important modernization perspectives and changes in educational work;
• to develop skills in initiating, carrying out and evaluating educational development projects.

Module 3: Socially Disadvantaged Groups. The module is designed specifically for SSP employees and consultants and focuses on criminality and prevention.
- Survey and insight into theories of crime and how crime can be prevented in society, groups, individuals and locally;
- legal regulation and legislation in the area and the importance of their administration.

The curriculum includes the following:
The goal is for participants to acquire knowledge about:
• key theories and concepts about the special needs and living conditions of socially disadvantaged groups;
• method development in social education work with these people.

Content
Theories, methods and concepts regarding:
• the living conditions of various target groups;
• various social education measures;
• various lifestyle problems;
• social psychiatry

Module 4: Normality and Deviation in Modern Society. The module is designed specifically for SSP employees and consultants and focuses on exclusion and inclusion. The module provides insight into young people's moral codex, criminality and the impact of sanctions. Trends in social disruption, new problem groups, changing family patterns and their challenges to the welfare state are considered critically. Participants learn to take an exploratory approach to the food-chain discussion in relation to gangs and groups, work with ethnic minorities and discussion of the dubious concept of 'social inheritance'.

The curriculum includes the following:
The goal is for participants:

- to acquire knowledge of key educational sociology theories, concepts and methods about inclusion and exclusion mechanisms in welfare society;
- to acquire insight into the history, development and function of the concept of normality, as well as learning the main theories and concepts of the relationship between normality and deviation.

Content

Theories, methods and concepts of:

- the influence of modern society on educational sociology;
- the history, development and significance of the concept of normality;
- various approaches to integration;
- the relationship between normality and deviation;
- deviation theories.

Module 5A (elective)

Counselling and Supervision as a Personal Qualifying Learning Process. This module is designed specifically for SSP employees and consultants and focuses on cross-sector, inter-disciplinary cooperation.

- A theoretical approach to the meaning and content of supervision and counselling seen in a social development perspective and positioned within various learning theories;
- clarification of the participant's own values and ethical dilemmas.

Competence goals

The goal is for participants to acquire insight into:

- project concepts as well as counselling and supervision concepts;
- learning process theory in relation to the process of counselling and supervision and develop the skills to
- plan and make process analytical deliberations about specific project counselling and supervision processes;
- reflect on their own position as project counsellor or supervisor, including the extent to which practice has been self-taught.

The curriculum includes the following:
The goal is for participants:
- to develop insight into counselling and supervision as a personal and professional learning process;
- to acquire knowledge about learning processes;
- to develop competences in order to
- lead and analyse counselling and supervision processes with insight into one's own position and that of other participants,
- reflect on counselling and supervision in social and historical contexts related to power, interests and ethics;.
- plan and analyse counselling and supervision processes on the basis of knowledge about learning processes.

Module 5 B: Conflict Resolution (elective). This module is designed specifically for SSP employees and consultants and focuses on cross-sector, interdisciplinary cooperation.

The goal is for participants:
- to be able to place various methods of conflict resolution in relation to basic values, views on humanity and society and subsequent understanding and attitudes to conflict;
- to develop on this basis the skills to resolve conflicts in various contexts, including negotiation/mediation
- to have a varied and critical attitude to various conflict resolution methods as well as to develop methods for personal practice.

The curriculum includes the following:
The goal is for participants:
- to acquire knowledge and understanding of attitudes to conflicts and conflict resolution;
- to have the opportunity to reflect on their own reactions in conflict situations and to receive personal feedback;
- to develop an awareness of dialogue based on respect and acknowledgement as a means in change processes and conflict situations;
- to develop competences that will spur development of a constructive conflict culture in a professional work-related context, such as:
  - skills in concrete conflict resolution, including negotiation/mediation;
  - skills in testing, evaluating and reflecting on various methods of conflict resolution in practice;
  - skills in incorporating ethical, interest- and power-related perspectives and using this understanding to act as a supportive third-party in a conflict;
  - skills in supporting and counselling people in conflict by working with conflict understanding and resolution;
  - skills in working with own personal learning processes regarding understanding and resolving conflict;

- skills in seeing various methods of conflict resolution in relation to basic values, views of humanity and society and subsequent understanding and attitudes to conflicts;
- skills in conflict resolution in various contexts, including negotiation/mediation, on the basis of the above;
- skills in acquiring a balanced view and being able to critically reflect on the various conflict resolution methods as well as develop methods for personal practice.

Content
- View of humanity and society in dealing with conflicts;
- understanding, analysis and dynamics of conflict;
- charting the roles of the various parties to a conflict – including the role as an involved or third party;
- communication: the language of conflict – verbal and nonverbal;
- active listening and sympathetic dialogue;
- conflict resolution methods, including negotiation/mediation between few parties, in groups, between groups and in conflicts to which the participant is a party;
- re-establishing processes between few and many people;
- ethical considerations and dilemmas in various methods of conflict resolution.

3. Process Consultant Scheme

In 2003, The Danish Crime Prevention Council (DKR) decided to establish an external consulting agency to help develop the quality of SSP cooperation. The goal was to provide consulting support to local authorities and police districts in their crime prevention efforts, based on the tasks and organization already established.

The local authorities could ask for consulting help:
- to set goals and methods for future SSP cooperations based on the local authority's existing form of cooperation and initiatives in the crime prevention area;
- to make goals and objectives more concrete;
- to define target groups more clearly;
- to identify organizational development needs;
- to identify method development needs, and
- to design evaluation schemes.

To handle the task, DKR decided to deploy consultants with wide experience in SSP work and made sure they represented a good geographic spread. Consultants agreed to devote 200 hours a year to the scheme, divided evenly between preparation time and actual face-to-face meetings.

DKR arranged a short training session for consultants, among other reasons in order to create a sense of fellowship among the consultants and to provide them with professional project management tools.

The process consultant scheme was conducted as a pilot project in 2003 and 2004, and an evaluation report was made in January 2005.

DKR decided to continue the scheme on the basis of the evaluation. It was also decided that future work would be targeted at the challenge of establishing/continuing SSP cooperation in the new local authorities (a concentration of many local authorities into fewer but larger entities as of 1 January 2007).

DKR currently has six consultants from all over the country involved in the scheme and is planning to add two or three more to it, preferably from the large local authorities that have experience with organizing interdisciplinary teamwork.

The common ground of the present consultants is their wide experience with SSP work in the local authorities. Aside from that, their backgrounds are diverse: some are teachers, some are engaged in after-school programmes and still others have no particular background in social services. As mentioned, DKR arranged a short training course for consultants, a copy of which is enclosed. In this connection, consultants were given a compendium in project management.

Paul Ekblom

Status Report United Kingdom - Crime Prevention Training in the UK: A Brief Review

1. Introduction

Much of what is described in this chapter is ephemeral. Crime prevention and crime prevention training in the UK have been subject to continual change throughout the last quarter of a century (though that change cannot always be regarded as improvement). Over the last few years the changes have been more rapid, and perhaps more wide-ranging, than usual. In late 2007 we may, or may not, be on the point of a major transition in the organisational structure of the delivery of training, if not necessarily in the content of that training. In order to be of most use to colleagues responsible for development of training in other countries, and more particularly as a contribution to the Beccaria Project, this description of the state of crime prevention training in the UK today is preceded by a brief historical account of how we came to be where we are; and followed by some more generic observations on the state of crime prevention training, and how it needs to progress if it is to serve its purpose of improving the scope and quality of performance of practitioners.

It is worth noting at this point that the meaning and scope of the term 'training' is itself problematic. How does training relate to 'education', with which it is commonly bracketed? There are many ways by which the various kinds of knowledge, understanding, skills and values of crime prevention can be imparted from 'experts' to 'novices' or in continuing professional development, ranging from classroom teaching to expert coaching. Does *training* imply that we are interested only in a particular subset of these? If the focus is a narrow one on the development of a European Master's degree in crime prevention, the answer is probably 'yes'; but even the planning of this particular medium should take cognizance of the wider context of how practitioners acquire, maintain and develop their competence.

2. The past – a brief history of crime prevention training in the UK

Crime prevention in the UK has a long history; a brief resume is worth presenting for the perspective it gives on current developments, and for anticipating similar trends and cycles in other countries where prevention has only recently emerged as a distinct activity.

The stated purpose of the Metropolitan Police, founded in London in 1829, was one of preventing crime rather than reacting to it. However, for various reasons, this soon became supplanted by an enforcement-based focus on detecting and catching criminals. This latter approach does of course have a major role to play in crime prevention, but the Beccaria Project centres on what can be called 'civil' crime prevention. This can be defined as making changes in the real world beyond law enforcement and the penal system so that criminal predisposition, motivation, resources and opportunity are reduced (see Ekblom 2004). In the mid-1960s the police moved a little in this direction when they instituted specialist crime prevention officers (CPOs), who (among other things) advised householders and organisations about physical security and ran local publicity campaigns of the 'lock it or lose it' kind. This was accompanied by the development of appropriate training courses and the founding of the original Home Office Crime Prevention Centre at Stafford (which even possessed a 'crime prevention house' for officers to practise on).

The gradual adoption of multi-agency and partnership approaches to crime prevention from the mid-1980s led to the UK government's Safer Cities Programmes (running from 1988-96, in parallel in England and Wales, Scotland and Northern Ireland). Provision of education and training to the small city-teams involved in the Safer Cities Programmes in England and Wales started with ad-hoc presentations by Home Office research staff, and centrally-commissioned courses from, for example, Manchester University. It finished by outsourcing the work to grant-funded charitable organisations such as NACRO (National Association for the Care and Resettlement of Offenders) and Crime Concern, which developed large-scale regional training courses and guidance materials, and a service of advisors.

With the change in administration from Conservative to Labour in 1997, the multi-agency trend culminated in the Crime and Disorder Act 1998, which provided a statutory and compulsory basis for local crime and disorder reduction partnerships jointly led by police and local government. The trend was accompanied by a broadening of the agenda, and the agents, of prevention; a corresponding broadening of the scope of education and training; and some early assessments of practitioners' training needs (e.g. Home Office 1998) in terms of competencies and 'underpinning knowledge'.

The Crime Prevention College (subsequently, Crime Reduction Centre, CRC) moved to bigger premises near York and tentatively developed courses aimed not just at police, but at their local crime reduction partners. The arrival of the Internet saw the development, in the late 1990s, of the Crime Reduction website www.crimereduction.gov.uk, which assembled a great deal of guidance and other self-instructional material for practitioners, including a range of 'toolkits'. The 1998 Act also inaugurated the national Youth Justice Board, which among other things supports good practice in local Youth Offending Teams. Many of YOTs' activities are preventive; usually, of course, they are offender-oriented rather than situational.

From the mid-1990s crime reduction began to move onto the agenda of a wider range of departments of national government, including those responsible for housing and planning, social/economic regeneration, health, trade and industry, education, and social inclusion. Crime reduction also became joined-up both nationally and locally with action to tackle drugs problems, and more generally with 'local strategic partnerships' (non-statutory, multi-agency partnerships, which match local authority boundaries, and bring together at a local level the different parts of the public, private, community and voluntary sectors; allowing different initiatives and services to support one another so that they can work together more effectively).

While the scope of prevention became ever wider, the risk of dilution of expertise and loss of focus increased with it.

The national Crime Reduction Programme (1998-2003) saw an opposing trend, with its focus on evidence-based intervention. Here the intention was both to encourage practitioners and policymakers to draw, in their choice of project, on reliable impact evaluations of past preventive action; and to support further evaluations to expand the evidence base. Getting the evidence base in a suitable form for policymakers to use was the responsibility of the Home Office Research and Statistics Directorate, which encouraged and applied the Systematic Review approach to identifying what works and what is cost effective, developed by various academics such as David Farrington of Cambridge University through the Campbell Collaboration (www.campbellcollaboration.org/CCJG). On the practitioner side, the Home Office Research and Statistics Directorate introduced 'Development and practice reports' to supply more detailed 'how to do' information. At about this time, the concept emerged of crime prevention delivery as a distinct set of activities covering supply and creation of infrastructure, organisational development, information exchange procedures, and capacity-building through education, training and resourcing.

To cope with the growing complexity and amount of material to be organised, the Home Office, and the Police Service, started to explore the field of deliberate Knowledge Management, taking on various consultants to try to systematically acquire, assess, consolidate and disseminate what was known about crime prevention/ crime reduction and community safety. (Knowledge Management has also explicitly been taken on by the Youth Justice Board on behalf of local Youth Offending Teams, and the Renewal Network www.renewal.net). This ongoing work saw the beginnings of the 5Is framework for knowledge management of good practice described below. And enough crime prevention posts of various kinds now existed to support 'grassroots' practitioner associations, such as the National Community Safety Network www.community-safety.net (for practitioners in local partnerships) and the more specialist Designing Out Crime Association (for planners, police architect liaison officers and design advisers www.doca.net). These all have an interest in the professional development of their members, so they actively contribute to the specification of training, and in some cases supply their own.

Academic departments and academic spin-off companies (such as Perpetuity Group, originating from Leicester University) responded to the increasing interest in evidence-based approaches by supplying training at a range of levels, to be described in further detail below. In one case, the Jill Dando Institute (JDI) developed its own self-declared practical discipline, crime science, in a deliberate attempt to distance itself from academic criminology, basing itself at University College London, where there had been no prior research in that field.

Crime prevention (hereafter, for brevity, taken to include crime reduction and community safety) has always had a rather precarious position in UK policy priorities. Concerns about 'crime waves' periodically surface and, boosted by the media, engage politicians in self-exciting 'auctions' of ever more ambitious and costly policies focusing on 'cops, courts and corrections' (i.e. enforcement, detection and punishment). Crime prevention, like preventive medicine, is not a politically-appealing topic and tends to lose out in such circumstances. The street robbery panic of 2003-4 was no exception, and large amounts of public funds were drained from Home Office budgets to tackle the problem. Although problem-oriented and other preventive approaches were supported, the bulk of the funds went into police overtime. This state of affairs arguably contributed to the closure of the Crime Reduction Centre.

An independent review of CRC was carried out in 2004 (Home Office 2004). It recommended that the direct training and learning services which the Centre had been providing for police and other community safety practitioners should be discontinued, on the grounds that these services were 'not well enough resourced to have made a significant impact'. Investing more resources in direct training was – apparently – not an option given pressures on Home Office budgets as a whole. The CRC therefore closed in July 2005; officials with responsibility for oversight of training were moved to London, where work continued through the Crime Reduction website, a journal aimed at practitioners, and the IPAK knowledge management programme (described later). The Home Office aimed 'to work with the Justice Sector Skills Council to ensure that there are national standards for community safety training, which employing organisations can use as part of their normal approach to workforce development.'

What about the delivery of crime prevention training? A 2005-6 review of partnership provisions of the Crime and Disorder Act 1998 (Home Office 2006a) stressed the importance of partnerships to crime prevention, and re-emphasised the proposal for national standards of performance, but there was no mention of training. Nor (apart from references to 'dissemination of good practice') did training feature in the National Community Safety Plan 2006-2009 (update, Home Office 2006b).

Given the closure of the Crime Reduction Centre, one might have expected that here was an opportunity for NACRO and Crime Concern to fill the gap in provision, particularly for training of local government community safety officials working in crime and disorder partnerships. However, both bodies underwent a change in senior personnel at this time and the new heads both chose to lead their organisations away from 'broad-spectrum' prevention towards a stronger focus on dealing with offenders. (Crime Concern closed its Consultancy division in 2006 but does however continue to supply various training services for crime prevention practitioners, and the situation is apparently under review).

Responsibility for training police CPOs shifted to Centrex, the National Police Training School, responsible for most training courses available to police forces in the UK. In yet another organisational upheaval (of the kind familiar to observers of the British scene) Centrex was itself absorbed within the new National Policing Improvement Agency (NPIA www.npia.police.uk), which officially opened for business in April 2007. The intention is that the NPIA will, with the Home Office, adapt the National Intelligence Model (NIM) – the business model for policing in the UK – as an equivalent model for partnership working in crime prevention (see www.crimereduction.gov.uk/nim1.pdf for discussions of how NIM relates to problem-oriented approaches). And the biggest organisational upheaval of all – the splitting in mid-2007 of the old UK Home Office into the Ministry of Justice (including of-fender management, which covers prisons and probation) and the new, smaller Home Office focusing on security, policing and crime reduction – has yet to reveal its effects.

This historical overview brings us to the present day and accounts for the fragmented and confusing nature of the current situation in the UK. A longer-term perspective may eventually produce a deeper understanding of events and processes, which can supply clearer 'lessons from history' to governments of other countries. But much could be simply attributed to the peculiarly British tradition of 'muddling through' instead of detailed and systematic planning, combined with hyperactive political rearrangement of organisations in response to short-term pressures and panics. One lesson does remain clear however, and that is likely to be a univer-sal one. Civil crime prevention requires sustained funding, high-profile champions, 'political respect', continuity of staff and accumulation of knowledge and expertise that are protected from short-term political mood-swings and public obsession with catching and punishing criminals, without of course being immune from accountability or isolated from intelligent public debate. UK political institutions have so far failed to deliver these sustaining conditions for crime prevention, and the situation on crime prevention training is part of that failure.

The present state of affairs is hopefully transitional. In theory the Home Office's current vi-sion of a combination of 'free market, with national standards', and a concern with deploying the full range of media for imparting competence provides a way forward that is suited to to-day's ever-changing institutional world. Much now hangs on the promised development of standards, the realisation of the potential of the NPIA and the continued development and teaching of leading-edge concepts and processes in academia.

3. The present

Preparation for this report involved a search of the internet for UK training providers and downloading of relevant material. A survey was then circulated to 30 apparent suppliers in April 2007. Only 8 responses resulted, ruling out quantitative analysis and limiting qualitative assessment. (The survey questions are available from the author). In addition, a discussion was held with a member of the Home Office team responsible for support of partnerships through the development and dissemination of effective practice. Based on this rather patchy information (which is perhaps symptomatic of the confused state of crime prevention training in UK), this section presents an overview of the demand for training, supply of training, and how quality assurance is pursued.

Demand for crime prevention training:

Who needs training?
The police, probation and youth justice services have an obvious and formal interest in crime prevention, whether through enforcement and punishment or broader approaches. Civil crime prevention seeks to intervene in an extremely wide range of causes of crime. Beyond specialist local authority community safety departments, an equally wide range of public and private institutions has some influence upon those causes in the real world. In the current political and policy climate, they and their personnel are often asked to take some responsibility for acting in a crime preventer role, whether acting in partnership or being mobilised in a more limited sense (Ekblom 2004). Consequently, they all require some level of crime prevention training. Dividing the preventer role into the three broad types identified e.g. by Clarke and Eck (2003), place managers include social housing managers, public transport managers, security guards and shopping centre/town centre managers; guardians of targets of crime include neighbourhood watch coordinators, victim support volunteers and yet more security guards; handlers of offenders include social/youth workers and voluntary mentors. At more remote levels from immediate crime situations urban designers, architects and planners require some training, as do top-level local council officials and elected council members. In most cases the training is optional; with the services having statutory roles in prevention, it is obviously mandatory. On the private security side, the UK government's Security Industry Authority requires that security staff, from nightclub bouncers to cash-in-transit guards, meet minimum qualifications before their company is licensed.

Levels of crime prevention activity requiring training
Content apart, crime prevention activity is carried out at a number of levels, each of which will have distinct training requirements. The Review of the Partnership Provisions of the Crime and Disorder Act 1998 (Home Office 2006a) envisaged both a strategic and an operational level of working in each locality, but it is possible to distinguish further such levels.
- Practice – the basic operational level. This includes analysing and solving crime problems (the basic activities of the preventive process as described by 5Is or SARA), and conducting crime risk assessments and crime impact assessments (Section 17 of the Crime and Disorder Act 1998 requires that local governments and their other local partners consider the crime implications of *all* the policy areas they are responsible for, from leisure services to waste collection; to support S17 activity, suppliers such as Crime Concern or Perpetuity Group provide specialist training to help local government officials and others to 'think crime').
- Delivery – the level at which infrastructure is created and maintained and human operational capacity is built. This relates to organisational structures and processes, information systems and flows, funding, setting up local partnerships etc, also to establishing appropriate staff career structures, organising and disseminating knowledge, training – and training the trainers. The latter is particularly important because there does not yet exist a large cadre of expert and experienced crime prevention professionals.

- Research and development – basic research on crime and its causes, and generation, tri-alling and evaluation of new activities. This helps to develop a range of capacities: operational, innovative and evaluative, by educating and training new generations of researchers as well as transferring 'how to do' knowledge by creating 'process' toolkits on crime analysis, evaluation etc.
- Policy – the level of establishing and sharing visions, setting strategic priorities and resolving conflicts of interest.
- Governance – the level of designing structures and processes for public decision-making and action, including those which support partnership working and other forms of citizen and institutional involvement in crime prevention.
- Public understanding and debate – covering a range of political issues. These include fundamental priorities and how they are to be traded off (e.g. safety versus privacy), the relationship between effectiveness of prevention and social/criminal justice, the acceptability of interventions in practice, the fairness of distribution of preventive action in relation to the needs of different groups and sectors in society, and the establishment of supportive climates for action (for example awakening public expectation that manufacturers of cars or mobile phones should have some responsibility for reducing the crime committed against, or with, their products).

The above levels are not in any kind of 'geographical' order, with 'local' at the top and 'national' at the bottom. Each kind of activity needs to be undertaken, to a greater or lesser degree of sophistication, at local, regional, national and perhaps international levels. For example, a local partnership may need to engage its community in a debate about how to handle under-age drinking without interfering with adult enjoyment of alcohol. Or an operational project at national or even EU level may be required to tackle identity theft. As well as crime-specific skills and knowledge, and their level-specific equivalents, people working at each level need generic competencies for example in project management, which has often been identified as deficient in reviews of implementation failure (see various papers in Knutsson and Clarke 2006; Wikström 2007 and Ekblom 2007 in press).

Supply of training

Crime prevention training in UK is available at a number of levels, ranging from one-day introductory courses for Continuing Professional Development to Masters degrees (e.g. the Masters in Crime Science at JDI UCL www.jdi.ucl.ac.uk and, most recently, the Professional Doctorate in Policing, Security and Community Safety at London Metropolitan University www.londonmet.ac.uk/pgprospectus/courses/policing-security-and-community-safety.cfm This course aims to produce professionally competent and informed practitioners who have a sophisticated understanding of wider policing theories and advanced research skills and abilities.

Training providers are equally diverse, reflecting the current free market (alternatively 'free-for-all' or even 'free-fall') situation.

- Universities include those already mentioned plus Leicester, University of the West of England, Glasgow, De Montfort, and the Open University (universities teaching criminology degrees without a strong practitioner emphasis have not been listed, but some of these departments/courses are obviously attended by practitioners in their own career development). Most of the departments involved are criminology or wider social science-based, but the JDI, reflecting its distinctive crime science orientation, is in the faculty of Engineering at University College London.
- Charitable organisations include the formerly broad-spectrum NACRO and Crime Concern, as mentioned; and others with a more specialist interest – for example the Suzy Lamplugh Trust which focuses on personal safety training, especially at work or on the street.
- Practitioner organisations/associations – for example the Designing Out Crime Association, and the National Community Safety Network of England and Wales, and the Scottish equivalent arrange conferences and seminars to update and inform members, but no formal training courses. The Association of Chief Police Officers organises an annual training/briefing conference for police Architect Liaison Officers and Design Advisers.
- Larger local government community safety departments (which may contain as many as 30-40 staff) may organise their own in-house training, and/or buy in customised courses from other service providers.
- The Metropolitan Police Service in London provides its own partnership training courses to London Boroughs based around a home-grown problem-solving model.
- Private consultancies such as Perpetuity Group (a university spin-off company with an emphasis on commercial security) and Evidence-Led Solutions provide off-the-shelf and customised in-house courses to local government departments and commercial clients.
- National Government organisations continue to supply various services. The Home Office (England and Wales) supports the Crime Reduction Website on behalf of a wide consortium of practitioner interests. The National Policing Improvement Agency was established on 1 April 2007, to deliver training and leadership programmes, develop and apply the latest policing doctrine, standards and best practice, and support the development and delivery of information and communications technology. Its 10-day Crime Prevention Learning and Development Programme is available to both police and crime prevention partner agencies and modules include: crime prevention principles, security products, site surveying, information gathering and sharing, multi-agency problem solving/ partnership working, counter terrorism, initiating and running a crime reduction project, and relevant legislation. An additional specialist 10-day course covers Designing out Crime. NPIA now has responsibility for the UK involvement in CEPOL, the EU Police College. In Northern Ireland, the Introduction to Community Safety is a vocational course for local practitioners delivered by five further education colleges.

Location of training ranges widely. It includes university campus; distance learning (especially with the Open University, and the University of the West of England) and self-instruction by website (www.crimereduction.gov.uk); national/regional seminar or conference programmes on an ad-hoc basis (e.g. Designing Out Crime Association, National Community Safety Network); courses delivered on-site where outside trainers go to the client's workplace; or courses taught in-house by specialist departments of the organisation such as a large police force.

Specialisation of training unsurprisingly caters for different ranks or grades (for example general police training at Masters level tends to cater for young, middle-ranking high-flyers), and for different areas of expertise, as with specialist training for Architect Liaison Officers/ Design Advisers, or for Restorative Justice. Private security training tends to exist in its own world, with the exception of Perpetuity Group, which attempts to span the divide between commercial and public practice.

There are several poles or axes of course orientation. Some are criminal justice-based, others focus on law enforcement and detection, civil prevention/community safety, or private security/risk management. Many are sociological (social control, governance), others psychological and/or situational. Few cover the entire field so the choice of which course to attend already leads the client towards some particular, restricted, perspective.

Organisation of knowledge for training
Organisation of knowledge and skills, to facilitate their transmission by training, takes a range of forms.

Case studies of good practice (nowadays usually accompanied by some kind of impact evaluation) are the basic feedstock of all other forms of knowledge.

Causal frameworks facilitate understanding of the causes and risk factors for crime, and awareness of the range of preventive interventions which practitioners can make in these causes. Frameworks include the Crime Triangle (target, offender, location) used widely in situational prevention, and the more detailed Conjunction of Criminal Opportunity (CCO) which aims to bridge the divides between situational and offender-oriented approaches, and between civil and enforcement/justice-based prevention. Each framework is accompanied by its corresponding Process model for doing prevention: SARA (Scanning, Analysis, Response, Assessment) and the once again more detailed 5Is (Intelligence, Intervention, Implementation, Involvement, Impact). Crime Triangle/SARA are supported at www.popcenter.org and CCO/5Is at www.designagainstcrime.com/web/crimeframeworks.

Toolkits cover both individual types of crime problem (such as domestic burglary) and preventive processes (such as partnership or evaluation). Most of these are found on the Crime Reduction website www.crimereduction.gov.uk but independent ones also exist – notably the guide by Clarke and Eck (2003) on crime analysis, published by the UCL Jill Dando Institute with Home Office support and widely translated. The JDI also supports the specialist field of research and practice in crime mapping.

Systematic (Campbell) reviews of the cost-effectiveness of various crime prevention interventions (such as street lighting, and CCTV) have been commissioned and published by the Home Office, but these tend to produce very high-level, generic assessments which are suited to the guidance of policy, but not of delivery or practice. The main reason for this on the practice level is that crime prevention is highly context-sensitive – what works in one place cannot be guaranteed to work in a different location, without careful customisation and a focus on the underlying causal mechanisms (Tilley 1993; Ekblom 2002a; Wikström 2007). On the delivery level, detailed knowledge is also needed to guide the establishment of the right infrastructure to help practitioners as individuals, and the organisations in which they work, to perform sufficiently well to realise the theoretical potential of the interventions.

Home Office research publications in the series 'Development and Practice Reports' have attempted to meet this need for greater detail on an ad-hoc basis; but a more systematic approach to collecting, assessing, consolidating and disseminating practice knowledge has been under development since around 2004. IPAK – Improving Performance through Applied Knowledge – adopts the mechanism-based approach just described. It is described at www.crimereduction.gov.uk/ipak/ipak01.htm . The rationale is that practitioners don't just need to know what works but also how and why something works if they are to understand and use the information effectively. IPAK assembles:

- Examples of effective practice
- Knowledge about crime and crime types
- Tacit knowledge (Tilley 2006) – knowledge about how something was done (know-how), such as working effectively with elected members or other partners – much of this extracted using the 5Is framework
  www.crimereduction.gov.uk/ipak/evidencebase/burglary005.htm The IPAK team is currently developing a methodology using burglary as a pilot
  www.crimereduction.gov.uk/ipak/evidencebase/burglary000.htm , evaluating this, then rolling out to other crime problems.

Quality assurance of training
Especially in a free-market situation, quality assurance of training is an important issue. At one level, quality assurance relates to the quality of the underlying evidence base which the training draws on – already covered in the section immediately above. At another level, the content, level and teaching/learning quality of the training courses themselves requires monitoring. In the UK, academic quality assurance (which applies to Masters-based courses for example) is covered by the Quality Assurance Agency for Higher Education (QAA, www.qaa.ac.uk). At the practitioner level, an important national player is the organisation *Skills for Justice* (www.skillsforjustice.com).

Skills for Justice is the 'sector skills council' covering all employers, employees and volunteers working in the UK justice system (there are many other such types of council, covering other areas of professional work). It provides support to enable the justice sector to:

- Identify its current and future learning needs;

- Engage more effectively with learning providers in order to meet these needs with high quality development programmes;
- Link acquisition of learning to reputable and valued qualifications.

Skills for Justice works in tandem with *Skillsmark* – a quality mark for learning and development in the justice sector www.skillsmark.co.uk. Skills for justice operates through four main work programmes:
- Engaging with and influencing employers, government departments and all key partners;
- Understanding and articulating clearly the current and future skills needs of those working in the Justice sector;
- Developing tools and services to improve the skills of the workforce, working with employers, learning providers and individuals;
- Implementing practical solutions to improve the skills of the workforce, working with employers, learning providers and individuals.

4. Performance – some reflections on training issues. A critique of the UK training situation

A number of problems have become apparent with UK training in crime prevention, problems which have contributed significantly to the phenomenon of implementation failure. This has haunted UK (and other) government attempts to roll-out, or mainstream, preventive action by replicating individual 'success story' projects (see for example Ekblom 2002a, 2007 in press; various papers in Knutsson and Clarke 2006).

We have already seen the fragmented nature of supply in the UK, the retreat of some major suppliers and the long, ongoing, pause before any strategic overview of the training requirements of practitioners is re-established and implemented. This has been compounded by a failure to systematically differentiate between knowledge and skills needed for the practice, delivery, policy levels etc distinguished above; and between requirements for conducting these tasks at different geographic levels.

Added to this has been a perennial lack of a common vision of crime prevention, community safety and related concepts. In particular, there remains considerable confusion about the relationship between crime prevention and justice (see for example Ekblom 2004) and in practice, Skills for Justice (as its name implies) does not properly cater for crime prevention/community safety.

Still more fundamental is the continued lack of interest in establishing a clear conceptual framework and clear language with well-defined and consistently-related terms to cover the field (Ekblom 2000, 2002a, 2002b, 2006). Working definitions of concepts such as community safety, devised initially by a group representing diverse professional disciplines and stakeholders (see www.designagainstcrime.com/web/crimeframeworks for the latest version) have been available since the inception of the Crime and Disorder Act 1998 (although infamously, the government minister responsible at the time for the act and its guidance said that he didn't want definitions). But although widely cited, neither this, nor any functional equivalent appears in the National Community Safety Plan (Home Office 2005) or its update (Home Office 2006b). Instead, the meaning of community safety struggles to emerge through a range of themes such as 'Making communities stronger and more effective', 'Further reducing crime and anti-social behaviour and building a culture of Respect', 'Creating safer environments' etc. The concepts overlap, are at several different levels, and are expressed in diverse discourses – so the end result is more like a Chagall painting than a technical blueprint. This cannot provide an adequate foundation on which training requirements can be identified, and training itself delivered.

This unwillingness to develop and apply definitions is perhaps part of a wider Anglo-Saxon anti-intellectual tendency in the public and political sphere, combined with an antipathy towards centralised direction (which is not necessarily a bad thing). But it also draws on a more specific, patronising view of practitioners as capable of understanding only the simplest ideas/methods. (One former director of a major crime prevention training organisation once said to me that all you could hope to convey to practitioners was a few simple slogans).

The Crime Reduction website, in its Learning Zone, contains an eclectic pot-pourri of different frameworks and models of prevention, leaving it to every new reader/practitioner to attempt to find their own path and create their own conceptual structures from the tangle. Most textbooks on crime prevention likewise lead the reader through a maze of specific theories and fail to synthesise them. The individual theories, such as Routine Activities Theory (Cohen and Felson 1979) and Cornish and Clarke's Rational Choice Theory (1986), are indeed simple, but again each practitioner has to struggle alone to build their own synthesis. Instead of the organised and penetrable complexity of a structured schema of concepts and knowledge, we have simplification and eclecticism of individual items which, piled in a disorderly heap, produce the opacity and confusion of a large junk sale.

As I have argued before (Ekblom 2006, 2007 in press), crime prevention is an extremely complex set of activities, and the frameworks, concepts and language used by practitioners, delivery managers and so forth must be sufficiently complex in themselves to efficiently handle that complex reality. Dumbing down and fragmenting the concepts to facilitate their communication, does not ultimately help performance, if what has been communicated is too simplistic to deliver successful crime prevention.

Training – rising to the challenge
Both crime and its prevention pose particular challenges to practitioners and thus to their training requirements. 'Ordinary', everyday crime is hard enough to tackle, but further challenges to those who seek to prevent crime come from the fact that many crimes are complex and sophisticated; criminal behaviour is persistent, invasive and progressive (including cor-

rupting the systems of crime control themselves). Many criminals are adaptive and durable, entrepreneurial, innovative and well-resourced, and increasingly dispersed and invisible as informal networks rather than clearly-structured gangs (Ekblom 2005a).

Crime prevention makes several kinds of demand. Data and theories need skill and knowledge to collect, analyse, interpret and use. Intervention mechanisms work at many levels – individual, interpersonal, group, community, cultural – and over different time and spatial scales. Implementation is complex – there are 'troublesome tradeoffs' between crime prevention and aesthetics, privacy, fire safety, convenience, sustainability and the ethical dimension. Replication of good practice can't be achieved by applying readymade cookbook solutions – it is far more like innovation which requires a combination of generic principles and practical methods to attune actions to new contexts. Crime prevention professionals usually have to work through many other people/organisations, alerting, motivating and empowering *them* to implement the intervention. This requires a further set of social and administrative skills. And evaluation is hard to do well – even to do well-enough to usefully contribute to the body of reliable good-practice knowledge.

In sum, the kinds of knowledge and skill needed by crime prevention professionals cover the following areas:
- Know crime – definitions;
- Know-about crime problems – nature, patterns, trends, causes, consequences, offenders;
- Know-what works to reduce crime;
- Know-how to put into practice;
- Know-who to involve in partnership or mobilisation;
- Know-when to act;
- Know-where to distribute resources;
- Know-why - symbolism, values, politics, ethics.

Know-how brings all these forms of knowledge and skill together in practical application. The one process model for doing crime prevention that has explicitly been designed to cater in detail for these topics, and to reflect the challenge of replication by operating on the twin levels of principle and method, is the 5Is framework (Ekblom 2005b and see also www.designagainstcrime.com/web/crimeframeworks).
- Intelligence
- Intervention
- Implementation
- Involvement
- Impact

I suggest (albeit immodestly) that this framework (or some future collective development of it) can supply the sophisticated, inclusive and adaptable process model required to give direction, structure and depth to crime prevention training. But whether or not this offer is accepted, a collective exercise is needed to develop a range of agreed definitions of terms linked together in a systematic and consistent glossary. One example of an attempt to do this, albeit in the rather specialised field of design against crime, is in Ekblom and Sidebottom (2007). Two illustrations from this glossary (which will be kept up to date on www.designagainstcrime.com/web/crimeframeworks) are as follows:

- Crime prevention:
  - o Reducing the risk of criminal events in terms of their probability of occurrence and consequent harm, by intervening in their causes
- Security adaptation:
  - o A security feature deliberately designed to make a product [such as a mobile phone] more secure against the risks typically to be encountered in its expected habitat or risk environment.

All this has implications for training. We need to be able to train up high-level professional consultants, well-versed in generic principles of CP and capable of innovating/improvising – not technicians with a limited repertoire. This level of skill and knowledge cannot be 'taught' solely in a classroom or over website – it requires practical, hands-on experience, tutoring by experienced professionals with an ability to articulate and assess tacit knowledge and apply evidence-based principles. In turn, this requires a high level of investment in training and other infrastructure needed to give a high yield in performance.

But for crime prevention to succeed, training is necessary but not sufficient. It must be accompanied by, and must be consistent with, the wider delivery context - especially the career structure and rewards for professionals, and wider organisational structures and processes. The developments in the UK described at the end of Part 2 above give some cautious grounds for optimism. But only time will tell.

References
Cohen, L. and Felson, M. (1979) 'Social Change and Crime Rate Changes: A Routine Activities Approach.' *American Sociological Review* 44:588-608.
Cornish, D. and Clarke, R. (1986) *The Reasoning Criminal.* New York: Springer-Verlag.
Ekblom, P. (2000) 'The Conjunction of Criminal Opportunity - a Tool for Clear, 'Joined-up' Thinking about Community Safety and Crime Reduction' in Ballintyne, S., Pease, K. and McLaren, V., eds., *Secure foundations: Key issues in crime prevention, crime reduction and community safety.* London: Institute for Public Policy Research.
Ekblom, P. (2002a) 'From the Source to the Mainstream is Uphill: The Challenge of Transferring Knowledge of Crime Prevention through Replication, Innovation and Anticipation.' In: N. Tilley (ed.) *Analysis for Crime Prevention*, Crime Prevention Studies 13: 131-203. Monsey, N.Y.: Criminal Justice Press/ Devon, UK: Willan Publishing.
Ekblom, P. (2002b) 'Towards a European Knowledge Base' and 'The 5Is: Experimental Framework for a Knowledge Base for Crime Prevention Projects' in *European Crime*

Prevention Conference 2002, vol. 1: 62-97. Copenhagen: Danish Crime Prevention Council. www.designagainstcrime.com/web/towards_european%20_k_base.pdf

Ekblom, P. (2004) 'Shared Responsibilities, Pooled Resources: a Partnership Approach to Crime Prevention', In P. Ekblom and A. Wyvekens, *A Partnership Approach to Crime Prevention.* Strasbourg: Council of Europe Publishing.

Ekblom, P. (2005a) 'How to Police the Future: Scanning for Scientific and Technological Innovations which Generate Potential Threats and Opportunities in Crime, Policing and Crime Reduction', in M. Smith and N. Tilley (eds.), *Crime Science: New Approaches to Preventing and Detecting Crime.* Cullompton: Willan.

Ekblom, P. (2005b) 'The 5Is Framework: Sharing good practice in crime prevention.' In E. Marks, A. Meyer and R. Linssen (eds.) *Quality in Crime Prevention.* Hannover: Landespräventionsrat Niedersachsen.

Ekblom, P. (2006) 'Good practice? Invest in a Framework!' *Network News,* Spring 2006. Chester: National Community Safety Network.

Ekblom, P. (2007, in press) 'Appropriate Complexity: Capturing and Structuring Knowledge from Impact and Process Evaluations of Crime Reduction, Community Safety and Problem-Oriented Policing', in J. Warren (ed.) *Community Safety: Innovation and Evaluation.* Chester: Chester Academic Press.

Ekblom, P. and Sidebottom, A. (2007) 'What do you mean, 'Is it secure?' Redesigning language to be fit for the task of assessing the security of domestic and personal electronic goods.' *European Journal on Criminal Policy and Research.* Electronically published at *www.springerlink.com/index/d8153x12n2wg75rg.pdf*

Home Office (1998) Introductory Guide to the Crime and Disorder Act. London: Home Office.

Home Office (2004) [untitled web page] *Review of Crime Reduction Centre.* London: Home Office. www.crimereduction.gov.uk/crimereductioncentre01.htm

Home Office (2005) *National Community Safety Plan 2006-2009.* London: Home Office. www.crimereduction.gov.uk/communitysafety01.htm

Home Office (2006a) *Review of the Partnership Provisions of the Crime and Disorder Act 1998 – Report of Findings.* London: Home Office. www.crimereduction.gov.uk/partnerships60.htm

Home Office (2006b) National Community Safety Plan 2006-2009 (update). London: Home Office www.crimereduction.gov.uk/communitysafety01d.pdf

Knutsson, J. and Clarke, R. (Eds.) (2006) *Putting Theory to Work: Implementing Situational Prevention and Problem-Oriented Policing,* Crime Prevention Studies 20. Criminal Justice Press, Monsey, New York, U.S.A.

Clarke, R.V and Eck, J. (2003) Become a Problem Solving Crime Analyst in 55 Small Steps'. London: Jill Dando Institute, University College London.

Tilley, N. (1993) *After Kirkholt: Theory, Methods and Results of Replication Evaluations.* Crime Prevention Unit Paper No. 47. London: Home Office.

Tilley, N. (2006) 'Knowing and Doing: Guidance and Good Practice in Crime Prevention', in J Knutsson and R Clarke (Eds.), *Putting Theory to Work: Implementing Situational Pre-*

vention and Problem-Oriented Policing, Crime Prevention Studies 20. Criminal Justice Press, Monsey, New York, U.S.A.

Wikström, P.-O. (2007) 'Doing Without Knowing: Common Pitfalls in Crime Prevention'. in G. Farrell, K. Bowers, S. Johnson and M. Townsley (Eds.), *Imagination for Crime Prevention: Essays in Honour of Ken Pease.* Crime Prevention Studies 21. Monsey, N.Y.: Criminal Justice Press/ Devon, UK: Willan Publishing.

Radim Bureš

Status Report Czech Republic - Crime Prevention Education and Training in the Czech Republic

1. Introduction

Crime prevention education and training is – unfortunately – not well established in the Czech Republic. This fact is even more serious when considering that several hundred full time men and women are engaged in crime prevention related activities.

One of the causes can be seen in the underdevelopment of Czech criminology as a study course[6] at any higher education institution. One cannot graduate in criminology at any Czech university. Becoming one of the few Czech criminologists requires studying a combination of the study programmes of Law, Sociology (Social Sciences, Social Work) and perhaps Psychology.

On the other hand we are witnessing a rather fast development in the area of other social sciences, like Sociology, Social Policy, Social Work or Social Pedagogy. Especially the development of regional universities which started after the political changes in the early nineties brought the development of new (or non-traditional) study courses often much closer to the practical needs. Crime prevention can benefit from this development as well.

Discussions on crime prevention education and training also very much depend on the definition of crime prevention itself. If we accepted a broader definition of crime prevention including also some police work or private surveillance or all aspects of situational prevention, we could get a slightly different picture. In this sense, formal education should include courses of study in Security or Crisis Management; these subjects are studied extensively, for instance at the Police Academy (see below).

2. Formal Education

Higher Education

There is only one institution of higher education, where crime prevention is taught as an independent subject: the Police Academy of the Czech Republic. Do not be confused by the name. Contrary to the use of this name in other countries, the Czech Police Academy is an institution of higher education with the majority of its students being civilians. (Schools for basic or

---

[6] The term "Course" is used in this text to describe an area of study you can apply for and you can graduate in. The term "Subject" is used to describe a single topic, which one can study throughout a year.

in-service further police training – often called "police academy" in many other countries - are called Police secondary schools or Police higher schools in the Czech Republic).

There is a department of criminology at the Police Academy. Within the Security course, you can take classes in both criminology and crime prevention. However, it is being considered to combine the two subjects in one degree programme. Students can use a textbook specially focused on crime prevention. The subject of crime prevention is practically oriented with emphasis on crime prevention management and the crime prevention system in the Czech Republic.

There are very few relevant subjects at law faculties. For instance, at the Prague Faculty of Law there is no separate criminology department; there is only a department of penal law. Within a single course of law, students can choose optional subjects like criminology or domestic violence.

The Law Faculty at Palacký University of Olomouc offers its students a solid social science background. Crime Prevention is touched both in the context of Criminology and of Sociology for Lawyers, with strong emphasis on social deviation.

Elements of crime prevention, with special emphasis on social crime prevention, are also taught at social sciences faculties or even educational faculties.

A study course perhaps getting the closest to the ideal crime prevention course as described in the Beccaria project documents can be found at a Hradec Králové University. At the Faculty of Education at Hradec Králové, there is a bachelor course "Social Pathology and Prevention" in the department of Social Pathology and Sociology. This study course reflects demands of agencies under the supervision of the Ministry of Education, Ministry of the Interior and Ministry of Justice for experts in prevention and harm reduction in social pathology. Social pathology is dealt with from the point of view of sociology, psychology, law and education. Developing skills to do research in the fields of social pathology and prevention is part of this course. There are also elements of managerial and educational training within this course.

At the University of Ostrava there is a study course "Social Policy and Social Work", which includes subjects like "Forensic Psychology in Social Work". The course is mainly devoted to penitentiary issues, but it also includes victimology and juvenile delinquency. Part of this study subject is field research in anti-social behaviour. Further there is a subject "Violence and Aggression as a Social Problem". This subject not only deals with the causes of violence but also with the prevention of violence and methods of dealing with violence (with special emphasis on bullying).

At the Prague Philosophical Faculty you can study Social Work, which include subjects like Social Pathology.

Secondary education

There is also secondary education and higher secondary education focused on security services with a special emphasis on crime prevention. This is provided by a private education company called TRIVIS – Public Law Secondary School and Higher Secondary School for Crime Prevention and Crisis Management. The company runs seven such schools in different regions of the Czech Republic. The main profile of the students graduating from these schools is to be future experts in the protection of people and property. They may work for private security companies, the municipal or the national police, but they are also prepared to work as experts in drug abuse prevention. The character of the school fosters situational prevention, but social prevention is not neglected either and recently even becoming more and more important.

The interest among students in this type of school is high, mainly due to the ever growing private security industry, and there are plans for a further expansion of the Trivis network. Focus on crime prevention is a direct sign that there is also a demand for crime prevention experts in the labour market.

3. Training

Training efforts with a comprehensive approach to crime prevention started in 1996, when the Czech Crime Prevention program started and the Crime Prevention Department at the Czech Ministry of the Interior was established. At the same time, a network of cities participating in the Crime Prevention Programme was developed. Cities participating in the program and eligible for governmental subsidies were obliged to appoint city crime prevention managers.

In 1997, a first training programme in crime prevention was developed for these managers. The training programme was based on a training-needs analysis carried out by a consultancy company. This needs analysis confirmed that management and organization training should be an integral part of the training programme since crime prevention managers should coordinate other agencies, establish and run partnerships, manage budgets, set goals and targets etc. Any successful crime prevention manager needs more than just experience in social work with clients or experience in policing. The in-house training programme lasted 14 days and consisted of 4 sessions.

The following topics were part of the training programme:
- Introduction to criminology, theory of crime prevention (situational, social and victimology);
- Roles and tasks of governmental ministries in crime prevention (Ministry of Labour and Social Work, Ministry of Education, Youth and Sport);
- Methods of crime prevention;
- Methods of social crime prevention;
- Methods of situational crime prevention;
- Informing citizens about crime prevention tools;

- Legal principles of police work and their role in crime prevention;
- Crime prevention activities within the national police force;
- Crime prevention activities within the municipal police force;
- Public administration with emphasis on the budgeting of crime prevention projects in municipalities;
- Assistance to victims;
- Fundraising – governmental and non-governmental financial sources;
- Good practice in crime prevention in some other countries;
- Introduction to management principles and methods.

The practical part of the training included the development of a city crime prevention programme and its mock presentation before the city council. The presentation was prepared in small groups so that participants could develop the programme in the discussion. Participants in the training programme also obtained a textbook prepared for this purpose. The whole training has been very successful and appreciated by participants.

Unfortunately, this training programme has never been repeated for reasons related to organizational, time and resource problems. Until today only very few participants are still active in crime prevention in municipalities.

In the subsequent years, several shorter training courses were prepared by the Crime Prevention Department of the Czech Ministry of the Interior. They usually lasted from 3 to 5 days. The topics were the same or similar to those the first programme, but they did not include the management segment. Also the main emphasis was placed on the detailed technique how to apply for governmental grants for crime prevention. The issue of planning and setting CCTV systems in cities was also emphasized.

One of the main obstacles to a more in-depth in-service training paradoxically seems to be the high staff turnover in the positions of crime prevention managers in cities. Because of this turnover, there was no willingness to invest in their training. It is hard to guess whether a hidden cause of this attitude is a disbelief in the quality of training or the conviction that managing a crime prevention project is an activity that does not require any special knowledge.

Crime Prevention Training for the Police
Crime prevention is not an essential part of initial police training; nevertheless, future police officers acquire some knowledge of crime prevention methods and approaches in different subjects (public order policing, traffic policing, and police reaction to domestic violence).

Recently, a new initiative started to arrange for standardised in-service crime prevention trainings for members of "preventive and information groups" of the Czech Police. These groups exist at all regional (8 of them) and district (75 of them) police directorates and of course at Police Headquarters. They are responsible for the coordination of preventive activities, for direct preventive activities (working at schools) and for communication with citizens and working with media. Press spokespersons are part of this group. The proposed course takes 3 weeks; the training is residential with three individual weeks during one year.

One week is focused on Crime Prevention. It consists of 5 sections:

1. Theory of Crime Prevention
Education goal: the participant understands the basic concepts of crime prevention and he/she is able to use them in the relevant context;
Topics presented: different components of crime prevention (primary, secondary, tertiary, social, situational etc.);
Duration: 2 hours.

2. The System of Crime Prevention in the Czech Republic
Educational goal: the participant is aware of the system of crime prevention in the Czech Republic, he/she is able to participate in developing local networks and establish links with relevant officials from the public administration.

Topics presented: National crime prevention programme at the local level and other national funding schemes, police participation in these programmes, initiation role of the police, granting schemes of regions and cities and possibilities for the police to participate in such granting schemes.
Duration: 5 hours

3. Crime Prevention within the Police and the Ministry of the Interior
Educational objective: he/she knows the legal provisions and internal regulations regarding crime prevention, he/she is acquainted with basic / strategic documents and knows the principles of funding crime prevention activities within the Ministry of the Interior and the police and is able to use this knowledge in practice.
Topics presented: Ministry of the Interior crime prevention programme, including the knowledge of tasks for the present period, national crime prevention strategy, running crime prevention projects within the ministry and the police, principles of developing crime prevention projects including budgeting.
Duration: 6 hours.

4. Police Protection of a Local Community
Educational goal: the participant knows the philosophy of community policing and other police approaches based on co-operation among the police, self-government and the public in general.

Topics presented: community policing, partnerships in community and region and the role of the police in it, principles of communication with local government and citizens, organization

of a problem-solving meeting, methods of involving citizens in the problem-solving, practical examples.
Duration: 4 hours.

5. Meeting, lecture, seminar, training, information handout
Educational objective: participant is able to organize and manage public lecture or meeting with citizens and he/she is able to produce informative hand-out.
Topics presented: different forms of presenting information, moderation of a discussion, structure of a meeting and a lecture, organization of a meeting, preparing leaflets and hand-outs, specificity of different target groups, managing of time.
Duration: 7 hours.

At the end of the training there is an examination in the form of a problem-solving task. Participants are divided into groups of 2 and already on the first day of the training they are given a topic for the final examination. They have the whole week to prepare for this examination. Topics for the final examination:
- Loan frauds,
- Frauds targeted at elderly people,
- Theft of noble metal,
- Burglaries to holiday homes,
- Marriages of convenience,
- Saturday night fever (risky behaviour of young people connected with visiting clubs on Friday or Saturday night).

There has just been one pilot run with a group of 12 participants for this brand-new (May 2007) training project. We spent quite a lot of time on this novel training project and its thorough and careful preparation (rather broad review of the curricula). The first run fully proved that it is a suitable training tool.

Non-Governmental Sector Initiative
In 2006/2007, EU funds could be used for a number of activities related to the development of social work, including prevention of social exclusion with specific emphasis on human resources development. The grant scheme was open to all suitable subjects, including NGOs.
In 2007, a Centre for Public Policy, a non-governmental organization (www.cvs.cz), received a grant to start special training courses in crime prevention for practitioners working on the prevention of juvenile delinquency. With a fundamental expert support from the Institute for Criminology and Social Prevention a textbook was written and the course was implemented for the first time in May 2007. The program also received input from abroad by Professor Tim Hope from the U.K.

This project differs from any others due to its heavy emphasis on criminology and theoretical principles of crime prevention.

76

Other Methods to Increase Knowledge of Crime Prevention

Besides formal education and in-service training, self-study plays an important role in enhancing knowledge in crime prevention.

There are three main sources of information related to crime prevention. At the basic level there are specialized pages in the monthly journal "The Police Officer" published by the Ministry of the Interior. The journal includes both basic governmental documents on crime prevention (such as governmental strategies, crime prevention programmes of the Ministry of the Interior or guidance on Community Policing) and a number of best practice examples from the Czech Republic and abroad. The journal mainly serves as a source of best practice, ideas and tips for their work to enthusiastic police officers (and there is a large number of them) who want to develop the preventive part of their work.

The next – more specialized – level is represented by the Information Service, which is published and distributed by the Department of Crime Prevention of the Ministry of the Interior. This newsletter is targeted at city crime prevention managers, police prevention officers, but also at mayors, probation officers and journalists. The newsletter publishes news from the crime prevention "community", research findings and expert articles on different topics of crime prevention.

Finally, for experts who are looking for more theoretical background information on crime prevention there are books published by the Institute for Criminology and Social Prevention of the Ministry of Justice. Their publication policy involves original research findings (recent studies on victimology and juvenile delinquency) and some original theoretical studies and translations. Translations tend to serve as a source of information to decision-makers in criminal policy and include, for example, studies commissioned by the European Commission in cooperation with the European Crime Prevention Network (EUCPN) or UN documents like UN crime congress proceedings or UN crime prevention guidelines.

Conclusion

The very recent time brought a number of new training initiatives in the area of crime prevention. These projects are well founded and of high quality, both with regard to their theoretical basis and the educational methods used.

Despite this development, we cannot be sure that finally crime prevention is on the right track to being a professionally-based activity. Experience shows that local administration and sometimes also governmental agencies tend to think that some activities do not require any professional preparation. In many areas of social life this tendency is prevented by a law setting educational and training requirements for certain professional positions. Medicine, Law or Education (not to mention the technical world) are good traditional examples. Public administration (especially at the local level) is a good example of the new development. There is no legal regulation concerning crime prevention and despite the efforts of a number of leaders in this area it is not predictable. For the time being we have to rely on voluntary initiatives of different agencies.

Otmar Hagemann

Status Report Schleswig-Holstein / Germany - Crime Prevention in Schleswig-Holstein

0. Introduction

The following is a status report about crime prevention in the north of Germany.[7] A central focus is an investigation of how the actors in this field are qualified and which institutions offer qualifications for crime prevention personnel.

Firstly, I would like to give an overview of crime prevention measures, programs and initiatives. This article will neither deal with crime prevention activities of city planners and architects nor with video surveillance and similar technical approaches. Prevention programs and activities concerning drug use and other addictions are also omitted because in that case delinquency is conceptualized as a health problem not as crime.

Secondly, I would like to discuss the crime situation in Schleswig-Holstein, because the remedies must be related to some problems or striking features. The third section will then deal with the question of qualification and it will include an analysis of offers of some institutions which could be thought of serving these needs. Finally, I would like to draw some conclusions related to the Beccaria initiative.

1. Crime prevention measures, programs and initiatives in Schleswig-Holstein

Schleswig-Holstein can be regarded as a pioneer in the field of crime prevention in Germany because it was the first federal state which had established a Council for Crime Prevention (Rat für Kriminalitätsverhütung) in 1990. This agency, modelled on Scandinavian examples, is still working. It coordinates practical activities in this field and offers assistance, for example by editing materials (i.e. PiT).

The idea has spread out from the regional level of the federal state (Bundesland) to the communal level and there are 87 local Councils for Crime Prevention [www.schleswig-holstein.de/IM/DE/InnereSicherheit/RatKriminalitaetsverhuetung...]. Before presenting the existing programs in Schleswig-Holstein we divide crime prevention into three levels:

<u>Primary crime prevention</u> is addressed to anybody. Probably the most common is the work with pupils in schools or even with children in kindergarten.

---

[7] The article is based on a presentation at the Beccaria conference in Hanover, April 28th 2007.

We are talking about <u>secondary crime prevention</u> if a specific problem has to be dealt with in the environment of an endangered or vulnerable group. For example, we know of groups, some of whose members have been identified as drug dealers or heavy users, frequently relying on violence or developing an ethics that is in contrast to socially acceptable values, i.e. extreme right-wing political ideas.[8] Working with potential offenders means preventing them from committing offences.

And finally, the term of <u>tertiary crime prevention</u> is used when aiming at known offenders and preventing recidivism or offering them alternatives both as general values / orientation and concerning behaviour in specific situations. This type of prevention is about forms of intervention when working with offenders in the aftermath of their offences.

However, this differentiation sometimes resembles more a heuristic tool than a selective system; furthermore, the following list of existing programs is not complete.

1.1 Programs and initiatives at the level of primary crime prevention
In 2001, the Ministry of Justice, Women, Youth and Family compiled a documentation of 93 prevention programs for children and young people, which differ very much in character, target groups and goals. This list was part of a response to a parliamentary question concerning the combat against right-wing extremism and hostility towards foreigners and especially the contribution of schools and institutionalised help for young people. The emphasis is seen on primary crime prevention, but the notion of crime prevention is partly rejected in this context. Instead, it is argued that we should talk about advancement of the culture of growth or the concept of supporting life competence, respectively (Schleswig-Holstein 2002: 6 with a reference to the 10th Child and Youth Report by the federal government in 1998). Among other things, the question of qualification needs for skilled employees in this field is formulated explicitly and trans-regional offers are demanded.

1.1.1 Communal councils of crime prevention
As already pointed out, Schleswig-Holstein was the first to invent the instrument of crime prevention councils. The biggest one is in Lübeck and has existed since 1992. There they had a budget of more than 300,000 € between 1995 and 2003, including research on public safety. I am working with the council of crime prevention in the town of Elmshorn, a suburban region close to Hamburg, where all the problems of modern society exist, such as social negligence, alcohol and illegal drug use, youth violence - especially between different ethnic groups - but also between individuals. The Elmshorn Council for Crime Prevention is a very active agency with a rather large group of volunteers attending its regular meetings. The

---

[8] Of course, the ideas themselves are not an offence. However, human rights are denied to other people and violence against opponents is frequently involved.

Council is divided into three working groups that deal with specific issues. Among the members of the youth crime prevention group, there are teachers and school principals, social workers, officials of local organisations like sports clubs, representatives of minority groups, policemen, local administration and even lawyers.

Similar councils operate in other towns. I have been informed by our free local weekly newspaper that my hometown also has such an agency and its work is introduced to the public via this medium and a very informative website (see www.kriminalpraevention.norderstedt.net). There are four active working groups dealing with young people, the elderly, immigrants and a city mall. Current activities deal with taxi drivers as potential witnesses and an anti-drug-week. Programs are described as "having a plan", assigning a kind of godfather to a young person in trouble. Whereas most of these elements look rather professional, my criticism concerns a questionnaire that was used to collect data from the citizens which violates a lot of basic methodological rules.

1.1.2 Prevention in a Team (PiT 1 and 2)
PIT is a prevention program consisting of learning modules which is carried out in school classes. Several modules aim at primary or secondary prevention and pro-social behaviour and help establish a positive atmosphere in school classes. Thus, it contributes to a reduction of delinquent behaviour among pupils. A team of adults - teachers and policemen, where appropriate also drug-counsellors - are being educated as a team and will shape the module together with school children between 11 and 16 years old. This program has been implemented in Schleswig-Holstein schools since 1996. Kase (2004 and 2005) stresses that it was repeatedly evaluated positively, which indicated effectiveness in the sense of the concept.

There are materials for four subsequent levels of work: 1. raising awareness of the consequences of delinquent behaviour by discussing the topics violence, theft and addiction, using concrete occasions and examples; 2. reducing fear of contact with the police; 3. personality development and promotion of pro-social behaviour; 4. improving the social climate in the school class to develop a sense of togetherness.

Before carrying out the project, the school conference is consulted to get support from the parents and other school classes. All modules consist of materials, checklists and agendas, which will allow even less experienced people to use them (see IPTS et al. 1996).

Some findings from evaluations: teachers and policemen express content. Objectives can, at least partly, be reached; the program is suitable for the purpose. They also feel empowered in dealing with phenomena of violence. The fourth element – *Samfund* (from Danish, meaning "behaviour in social relationships") – is seen as the most difficult one to implement. The atmosphere in the school, co-operation among colleagues and in the classes are crucial for its success. Role play sometimes involves overcoming a high threshold, but facilitates practicing new forms of behaviour. Teachers and pupils experience a more positive interaction and climate in the school class, with a significantly improved integration of outsiders and an improvement of the relationship between teachers and children. The program allows dealing with problems more openly, strengthening self-confidence and an improved conflict management. Fear of contact with the police decreases.

Similarly, in 2000 PiT 2 was developed for working with younger pupils between 6 and 9 years of age in elementary schools. It aims at social learning with the main emphasis on dealing with conflicts, because this is really a touchstone for social competence (see Kase 2005). For even younger children in kindergarten, the programs Faustlos (Fistless) and Faustlos plus, which are of American origin and adjusted to German conditions, are used (see Cierpka 2002). These also involve the parents.

1.1.3 Prevention activities of the police and related institutions
Beside the activities in the PiT program, the police themselves offer several things. The following websites might be interesting for young people. At www.time4teen.de, young people can find crime prevention tips written in the typical youth language (and without any explicit relation to police or other authorities). Another website can be found at www.polizei-beratung.de, where some brief articles give information on specific problems such as violence against children or against women. Furthermore, in the bigger police departments there are persons specifically responsible for youth matters.

1.1.4 Sport against violence (Sport gegen Gewalt)
Sport against violence, intolerance and hostility towards foreigners is a network of projects by the sports association of Schleswig-Holstein. In 1994, upon proposal of the political authorities and financed with the public budget, initially 40 project groups were founded - today there are 85 at currently 40 locations throughout the federal state. These groups meet regularly, most of them once a week. In addition, some one-day events are offered. Since 1998 the so-called Fair & Fun Tour has been carried out (cf. www.lsv-sh.de/fairandfun). Furthermore, integrative holiday camps and specific events are offered. There are between 30 and 40 (part-time) trainers (trained pedagogues), who work on the basis of a specific concept, but with the freedom to make individual arrangements. The concept is about creating meaningful leisure activities to deal with the given lack of orientation, egocentric thinking and conduct and increased acceptance of violence. Instead, positive values such as respect, peaceful interaction and fair play are promoted. This is accomplished by strengthening self-confidence, awareness for one's own body, caring for one's health and being critical of racism. Conventional types of sport like volleyball, soccer, table tennis or competitive sport from the Far East as well as more uncommon activities like floorball, hiphop or break dancing are offered. In the town of Lübeck, streetball and soccer-points have been established. The target group are predominantly young people, who want to try out new forms of sport. The aim is to motivate them to join sports clubs and develop some kind of commitment and involvement (see Hirschi 1969). The Sports Association of Schleswig-Holstein co-operates with schools, religious communi-

ties, public and private social organisations of youth aid, the police, unions, local authorities and other associations (see Pötzke 2006).

1.2 Programs and initiatives at the level of secondary crime prevention

It is in the nature of this approach that the following programs are much more focused on a specific problem or target group.

1.2.1 diba-ST (ST stands for safety training)

The former policeman (1984-1994) and self-defence expert Dirk Baasch has developed the so-called *diba-safety-training* and his company offers training both to police and justice personnel as well as to citizens, especially teachers and pupils. The training focuses on personality enhancement as well as purposeful strategic defence and communication. The diba-safety-training can be clearly distinguished from competitive sport and traditional self-assertion courses. There are group and individual training courses in modular form, an anti-violence-training for young offenders and also for adults, courses in conflict and crisis management (for example, behaviour in encounters involving knives and guns) and a train-the-trainer course (see www.diba-st.de).

1.2.2 Prisoners are helping young offenders

The main project was invented by inmates of the Hamburg prison for long-term sentences in Fuhlsbüttel. This group is still involved, but some modifications seem to have been made by the people using this project, i.e. a group from the city of Elmshorn. It is a sort of "scared into being straight" program, which is very much debated in the literature (see PSB 2006: 683).

1.2.3 KIK network against domestic violence (Kieler Interventionskonzept)

To begin with, KIK is a network of 14 regional coordination centres and 10 organizations (e.g. Ministry of the Interior, public prosecutor's office, association of women's refuges, women's initiatives) which are professionally faced with domestic violence and spouse abuse. It deals with police-registered cases only. Since 1999 the project has been covering the whole federal state.

One aspect of the KIK project is the use of personal protection orders to protect mainly female victims from male aggressors who are closely related to these women. These males can be evicted from their homes by the police and this intervention does not have to be requested by the women. However, this police activity is restricted to a period of 14 days (see Schleswig-Holsteinischer Landtag, Drs. 15/2077)[9], not implying a permanent removal from the household. If it should be necessary to have a permanent order for a person to keep a cer-

---

[9] In Hamburg, the period is 10 days, which can be extended to 20 days if the victim applies for court protection, see § 12 b Hmb SOG.

tain distance to another person, a civil court must issue this order. (see Gewaltschutzgesetz of 2001 (law of protection against violence) and specific state regulations).

Bettina Holst and Monika Frommel (2004) have evaluated the Kiel cases for the period from 1997 to 2003. They found an increase in cases of control by the police from 264 cases in 1997 to 748 in 2003. However, "only" 259 of these cases were classified as an offence (the differentiation between "offences" and "conflicts" was introduced in 2001). With seeking "stringent application of prosecution" there is a punitive aim in this initiative, whereas the victims themselves seem to prefer civil law procedures ("It was difficult to gain victims as witnesses in a criminal proceeding."). The program does not recommend mediation. This is mostly due to the usual outcome in court: in cases of conviction the penalty in most cases was a fine. According to Holst and Frommel, we do not find the usual pattern of sanctioning for re-offending, so they and other experts ask for more punitive sanctions. In 2003, 69 personal protection orders were imposed by the police (meaning eviction of the suspect from his/her home) plus additional claims by civil procedure. 28 of the accused persons had to take part in a social training program. This number has stayed nearly constant since 1997.

Whereas KIK primarily focuses on women, there is another network-approach exists for children that was started in Flensburg. The project *Schutzengel* (guardian angel) for Schleswig-Holstein is carried out with support from Kinderschutz (child protection). It is another program to create a support network for families living in difficult circumstances.

1.2.5 Präventionsbüro PETZE, Kiel

This advice centre of the voluntary agency "Notruf (emergency call) Kiel" focuses on sexual harassment and indecent assault involving girls and boys and has developed materials and prevention programs for use in schools. To name one example, there are different exhibitions aimed at teachers, parents, students and older pupils. PETZE offers qualification for teachers (see www.petze-kiel.de).

1.3 Programs and initiatives at the level of tertiary crime prevention

Whether the following programs can be classified under the notion of "prevention" or the term "treatment" seems to be more adequate is left to the reader since treatment always implies the prevention of recidivism, and prevention in a narrow sense of the word has failed already since here we are confronted with offenders.

1.3.1 Working groups against violence in schools

Working groups against violence in schools is a prevention initiative that aims at fast and concerted action between school, police, prosecution and court assistance in juvenile courts (JGH) to react consistently to deviant behaviour of pupils. Like in the case of KIK, the focus is on networking of professionals responsible for a certain case.

1.3.2 Anti-violence-training (by Scholz & Behrens from bfw)
Christian Scholz & Kathrin Behrens from bfw (an NGO of the unions mainly dealing with vocational training and advanced training courses but also very much active in prisons all over Germany) have developed a victim-centred anti-violence-training[10] for juvenile prisoners which they carry out regularly in the youth prisons of Schleswig and Neumünster (duration: five months, weekly from 3.30 to 7.30 p.m.). A course with a group of about 8 to 10 inmates will last several months and consists of several elements (presentation and analysis of one's biography, victim empathy, work on the offence and confrontation, negation of neutralisation techniques, coming to terms with one's deed and taking responsibility for one's own action, acquiring skills for conflict resolution). Additionally, they offer workshops on the issue of violence to schools, kindergartens and clinics and also other conflict trainings similar to diba.

1.3.3 Social rehabilitation of prisoners
There are various endeavours ranging from quite unspecific treatment for social rehabilitation in the prisons to certain aftercare programs. The NGO Ev. Stadtmission Kiel offers advice and help to prisoners who are preparing for release (accompanying inmates on temporary leave for job interviews or similar things); this support is continued after release on a voluntary basis (project Haftberatung, see www.stadtmission-kiel.de/193.php). It deals with questions of housing, employment, debt regulation and all the aspects in dealing with authorities (such as applying for identity papers, residential registration, and tax card). For inmates and ex-prisoners in Lübeck another NGO Resohilfe offers assistance specifically to Russian and Polish speaking prisoners (project Integrationsberatung, see http://resohilfe-luebeck.de). Both organisations also train volunteers for 1-to-1 social work.

Another initiative of managing the transition process from prison into freedom based on the concept of case work is currently in a development process supported by an NGO for the support of offenders (Landesverband für Straffällige) and the Ministry of Justice.

In 2006, the state of Schleswig-Holstein decided to spend nearly 3 million Euros for better work qualification of inmates in its prisons (see Landesregierung.Schleswig-Holstein.de, 15.4.2007); more details can be obtained from the Reso-Nordverbund, which involves the bfw and other organisations and is based in Bremen (see also webgate.ec.europa.eu/equal).

1.3.4 Packhaus
Since 1995 Packhaus (an advice centre of the NGO PRO Familia) offers therapy to predominantly male sex offenders who have to comply with a condition or against whom (criminal) proceedings have been started. Therapy is always on an obligatory basis. The concept in-

---

[10] This program differs somewhat from what Weidner has founded. Scholz & Behrens have also trained people who offer similar programs as mobile group work (see Kieler Antigewalt und Sozial Training (Kiel anti-violence and social training)).

cludes working on a detailed reconstruction of the offence, working out adequate strategies on how to cope with conflict situations and how to act when experiencing stress. It is assumed that people who interact in an acceptable way with themselves and others will not commit sexual assault. The aim of this work is to prevent recidivism (see www.packhaus-kiel.de).

1.3.5 Mediation

Mediation does not aim primarily at crime prevention, but evaluation studies found out that it has a preventive effect for participants if it is successful (see Morris & Maxwell 2001; Strang & Braithwaite 2000). The predominant form used in Schleswig-Holstein is victim-offender mediation. Although there are no comprehensive data, there is some indication that it is successful in most cases (see Koller & Hagemann 2007). Just recently, a project on family group conferencing inspired by the New Zealand and Belgian model has started in Elmshorn.

1.3.6 Diversion

Whether diversion should be listed under prevention activities is probably questionable, too. However, since the early 1920s we have known from Franz von Liszt that the best way to prevent youngsters from further offending can be not to impose any formal sanctions. Schleswig-Holstein is one of the pioneers in applying diversion and has even extended it to the police level.

2. The current crime situation in Schleswig-Holstein

In this section, I would like to identify the current problems to be dealt with regarding the crime situation in Schleswig-Holstein. Commonly, police statistics are used as data sources for this purpose. Alternatively, analysing conviction statistics will also make sense. Unfortunately, there is no recent statistical information based on victim surveys or self-report studies. As a nationwide source we should analyse the second periodic report on security in Germany which was published in 2006. There was a similar endeavour in Schleswig-Holstein referring specifically to the situation there. Criminal offences cover only one part of the problems.

Looking at police statistics, since 2003 a steady decrease in the overall crime figure can be noticed. In 2006, with 8,555 offences per 100,000 inhabitants, we had the lowest crime level in the last ten-year period.

Theft is the most common offence (46.0%) followed by vandalism (13.9%) and other property offences (13.5%). More serious forms of violence (3.1%)[11], robbery (0.7%), sexual offences (0.9%) and offences related to illegal drugs (3.4%) constitute only a small proportion

---

[11] This is the category "Gewaltdelikte"(violent offences). The proportion of dangerous and aggravated assault is 2.2%. The given figures do not add to 100% because categorization of the police statistics serves other purposes than this article. I have omitted specific migration-focused laws, insults, arson, offences against public order but also minor injury (which will add to more than 19%).

of police registered crime (see Police Crime Statistics of the Schleswig-Holstein police, 8.3.2007). Despite the positive impression one can get from police statistics, the Minister of the Interior called for extended and more intensive prevention efforts in kindergartens and schools. He mentioned some successful prevention programs – among them PiT and KIK. And he expressed his concern about right-wing violence, which is one of the few categories that have shown an increase. Other such categories are corporate crime (increase of nearly 23%) and computer crime (with an increase of approximately 10%).

Given all the problems connected with police statistics, it would be naïve to assume that we can derive the necessary preventive measures (needed for intervention) directly from this official estimation (statistical picture). Instead, we must take into account that safety and security are social constructions and so are the priorities of reaction. Several actors contribute to this social construction: the media, the police, other administrators and politicians, experts from science, parents and organisations for the protection of children, women's interest groups, victim support agencies, various non governmental organisations and charities. However, this discourse only rarely includes youngsters (see Magdeburger Initiative) and members of minority groups or (other) marginalized segments of society. Thus it is no surprise that crime prevention as a formal social control focuses on the least powerful social actors.

In general, dealing with crime prevention means to prevent young people from committing illegal or socially problematic acts. The victim perspective has the second place: protecting women and children against male violence. In the third place, there is currently a focus on elderly people, who are considered to be more vulnerable, especially when they live in care institutions or when they are targeted in their homes by swindlers (see Schleswig-Holsteinischer Landtag, 32. Sitzung des Sozialausschusses am 15.1.1998 on "violence against the elderly – prevention and intervention", 1998). Terrorism is becoming increasingly important on the agenda - at least on the state level, in the media and in parliamentary discussions.

Between 1994 and 2005, the number of convicted juveniles (14-18 years old) has increased almost constantly, whereas the number of young adults (18-21) and adults stayed almost constant. This may support the hypothesis that the offenders are becoming younger. However, keeping in mind that 8,555 offences were registered per 100,000 inhabitants, the rate comparable to convicts was 782 in 2005.

My assessment of the crime situation is supported by the statistical data and official assessment mentioned above, but it also captures some insights resulting from educating students of social work. After six semesters of theory they do a one-year internship (Praxissemester) in institutions of social work (i.e. youth welfare committee, probation service, advice centres, migration bureaus, schools and so forth). During this period, they spend one day at our university and each professor offers a kind of group supervision to support the transition from theoretical to practical work. This is a valuable resource in this context for it allows an insight into certain life-worlds that is not filtered by the media or politics.

2.1 Racism and threats from right-wing extremists

According to police statistics, there was an increase in the category of politically motivated crime, i.e. right-wing crime from 337 offences in 2005 to 510 offences in 2006 (more than 10% of them are classified as violent). At the same time there was a sharp decrease in left-wing crime (273 compared with 118).

We also know about such an increase in right-wing extremist violent offences (hate crime) from other German federal states. There are frequent conflicts between neo-nazis and "independent" people (*Autonome*) but also ordinary citizens. The program Sport against Violence addresses this issue, but only focuses on mere sympathizers or potential recruits. In Brandenburg, Helmut Heitmann has developed a tertiary prevention measure for the incarcerated neo-nazis (see Korn & Heitmann o.J.).

2.2 Juvenile misdemeanours and risky behaviour

Forms of risky behaviour among adolescents, including heavy drinking, use of illegal drugs and also risky forms of sexual behaviour, are common. Even illegal car-racing on public streets has been reported. This deviant behaviour neither appears in police statistics nor in the list of preventive measures. As far as drugs are concerned, there are specialised agencies and drug prevention programs. And the police seem to deal effectively with violations of traffic laws.

"Happy slapping" and other forms of violence occur among young males, sometimes including females, too. According to local information, this seems to be a problem in some schools. The PiT-program tackles questions of violence. Diba offers help to victims. Frequently spraying graffiti and tagging are seen as common problem of vandalism.

2.3 Integration of migrant juveniles

Sometimes the integration of migrants of the second ("Russians") or third ("Turks") generation seems to be more difficult than it was with their parents (see Schäfer 2004). Sport against Violence should help. Under the umbrella of the program "social city" (Soziale Stadt), some specific measures have been implemented in Mettenhof – a neighbourhood with a high proportion of immigrants. Young people participate in decision-making concerning their spare time activities, i.e. facilities for skateboarding have been installed and some youths have been appointed as persons in charge. This is symbolized by a kind of passport issued by the local youth welfare committee.

In addition Kücükkaraca presented activities of the NGO Turkish Community of Schleswig-Holstein at the "Northern regional conference for equal opportunities and against discrimination" in Kiel in June 2007. Migrant associations support issues such as inclusion in the labour market and the education system and do explicitly not focus on crime prevention.

2.4 Assaults on officials

This refers to acts violence and other forms of offence carried out by drop-outs and directed against members of the system – I would like to mention the behaviour of pupils against some teachers and, more frequently, the behaviour of clients of the welfare system towards clerks (diba offers help). Even though I do not know of any systematic data collection, information from anecdotal examples and from brief reports in the local newspaper show incidents of assault on officials other than policemen (i.e. agencies for employment seekers, social welfare offices, probation service, but also teachers and even sports referees).

2.5 Problems between children and adults

Without doubt there are some overworked parents and also parents who do not care very much about their offspring. This may result in violence against children or negligence (see Wetzels 1997). The youth welfare offices are obliged to offer help and to guarantee the well-being of the child, the more so if it is very young and cannot take action on its own. The *guardian angel*-networking project was established for this purpose.

When growing up, physical vulnerability on the side of the child may decline. However, adolescence is another challenge, both for the parents and the young people. Some youths may get out of control of their parents / educators. This may include anti-social behaviour, criminal activity or drug addiction. The state as guarantor of the well-being of a child is responsible to educate young people under 16 and assist young people under 18 if their parents are unable to do this. After the closed institutions for this age group have been abolished, now there is no institution to take their place; psychiatric hospitals refuse to accept these clients if they act violently. How can we prevent the exclusion of this group from nearly all social institutions without falling back to prison-like institutions?

2.6 Sex offenders

There are a lot of discussions about sex offenders, especially paedophiles – this may reflect a moral panic, using a small group of offenders as scapegoats for broader social problems (globalisation, diverse forms of risk). Since 1998, a new law has led to great changes, i.e. the establishment of a "socio-therapeutic" prison department in Lübeck. In 2006, more than 10% of all inmates were classified as sex offenders, although according to police statistics less than 1% of all offences in 2006 were sexual offences. Only 1.4% of all convicts were sentenced because of sexual offences.[12] Every sex offender who was sentenced to at least two years of imprisonment faces more impediments to regain his freedom or relief of regulations. On the level of tertiary prevention, treatment programs like SOTP may prevent recidivism. However,

---

[12] Similarly, in Hesse an increase in convicted sex offenders of more than 7% is reported, although crime in general had decreased, like in Schleswig-Holstein. Experts attribute this to a reduction in the size of the dark figure. In total 652 persons were sentenced there in 2006 because they had committed sexual offences (see Frankfurter Rundschau 1.8.2007).

not every offender charged with a sexual offence needs treatment, because in some cases the offences were committed many years ago, followed by a period of 10 or 20 years without recidivism (oral communication by therapists working in the prison).

2.7 Terrorism

Although not yet rooted in the every-day life of the Schleswig-Holstein citizens there are nevertheless some tracks of international terrorism leading to this federal state. In August 2006, a 21-year old Lebanese student from Kiel was arrested because of attempted bomb attacks on a train in the west of Germany on July 31, 2006. In July 2007, legal proceedings were taken against a 37-year old man of Moroccan origin from Kiel. He was charged with supporting Al Quaida and helping to infiltrate suicide assassins into Iraq.

The minister and the media are taking this subject seriously. As far as I know, there are no prevention programs aiming at certain groups, such as foreign students or migrants from Muslim countries.

Furthermore, we had some bomb threats in train stations or schools – some of them turned out to be bad jokes of youngsters. In my hometown we had a case of an eight-year-old school boy threatening others by claiming to have disposed a bomb in a school (of course, his identity was revealed <u>after</u> evacuating the school building and searching for the bomb without success).

3. Potential providers of crime prevention qualification

Section 1 dealt with measures and programs in place and section 2 compared the offers with what seems to be needed. Section 3 deals with the institutions where the required qualifications for the personnel can be obtained. Ideally, this is a kind of interface between science and interested citizens. Which opportunities do universities and private institutes offer to these people to become more informed about crime prevention?

This section is based on internet research and first-hand information provided by colleagues. I am including academic institutes, an intermediary level of organisations of the federal state (e.g. the police and administration) and some private training providers in Schleswig-Holstein. Because many inhabitants of Schleswig-Holstein are more oriented towards Hamburg than Kiel I also enclosed Hamburg universities. There is no guarantee that the following overview is comprehensive. I could not find any relevant experts, courses or projects at the universities in Flensburg and Lübeck, at private universities or at Helmut-Schmidt University, Hamburg.[13]

---

[13] No entry found when searching for "crime prevention" or "security" at Helmut-Schmidt Universität der Bundeswehr, Hamburg.

3.1 Universities in Schleswig-Holstein

The following portrays courses and programmes offered by universities in Schleswig-Holstein.

3.1.1 Christian-Albrechts-University Kiel

Monika Frommel teaches law students (including psychologists who study law as a minor subject); among other things, she is responsible for the subject of criminology. Heribert Ostendorf – one of the leading lawyers in juvenile law and an expert in juvenile crime (see Ostendorf 1997) – is very much involved in dealing with questions of crime prevention. Both of them are outstanding personalities in the field of crime prevention (several dissertations have been completed under their supervision, *Magdeburger Initiative* as an attempt to take young people seriously, evaluation of the KIK project). However, their students are mainly law students. Some of them complete an internship in the prison of Neumünster, but these are exceptions. Lawyers do not form a core group in crime prevention activities.

At the CAU, another distinguished expert, the psychologist Thomas Bliesener, is very active in this field and has specialized in criminal psychology, diagnosis, assessment and treatment of serious offenders, especially in preventing sexual offences. His team is cooperating closely with medical clinics and psychiatric and sentencing institutions working on treatment programs (tertiary prevention). He emphasizes that psychologists from his institute are explicitly qualified for jobs in the fields of prevention, intervention and justice (see www.psychologie.uni-kiel.de/entwpaed/arbeitseinheit.html).

To summarize, CAU has a lot to offer, but their target groups - lawyers and psychologists - do not represent the people who are active in the projects and initiatives most in need of this kind of knowledge.

3.1.2 University of Applied Sciences in Administration in Altenholz (FVSH Altenholz)

At the University of Applied Sciences in Administration in Altenholz, police officers are educated. According to the analysis of the personnel in the local councils of crime prevention and because of the various activities of the police itself they form a core group. Here we find a mandatory seminar in the curriculum dealing explicitly with crime prevention. Furthermore, a study programme in security management leading to a B.A. degree is offered as an extra occupational qualification for executive positions in security management. With reference to 9/11 it is stressed that we face new challenges in providing security for governmental agencies, businesses and organisations. Managers from all sorts of businesses form the target group – they may transfer their knowledge to the local councils because quite often local businesses participate. However, professor Dubbert (a psychologist, profiler) stressed that the content is very police-focused, meaning that the emphasis lies on target hardening and situational crime prevention, and to a lesser extent on social prevention, especially on secondary or tertiary prevention.

3.1.3 Kiel University of Applied Sciences

My own work at Kiel University of Applied Sciences focuses on teaching students who want to become social workers. This is an appropriate group in our context, since almost all of the mentioned projects involve social work. However, I am the only professor teaching sociology including deviant behaviour and forms of intervention and aftercare assistance for ex-offenders. Together with mediation, these can be conceptualised as criminological subjects – because criminology does not exist in our curriculum, nor does crime prevention. Students seem to ask for these topics only occasionally – especially after doing internships in institutions such as court assistance in juvenile courts, prisons, probation service and the like).

Furthermore, I have developed a victim-empathy training in the socio-therapeutic prison of Altengamme (Hagemann 2004).[14] Colleagues responsible for teaching law, health or youth work and offering seminars like "family assistance" also tackle some of the aspects in focus. But it is only every now and then that a question of crime prevention arises. Nevertheless, her research leads Raingard Knauer to the statement: "Viewed from the perspective of children support services, crime prevention needs the participation of the target groups, especially that of young people (see Knauer 2004).

To sum up: We are the only university for the education of social workers in Schleswig-Holstein, but the topic crime prevention is of marginal interest only.

3.2 Trans-regional institutions in Schleswig-Holstein

IPTS is the abbreviation for the Schleswig-Holstein Institut für Praxis und Theorie in der Schule (institute for practice and theory in schools) of the Ministry of Education. It offers further qualification for teachers, develops curricula and teaching material, is responsible for projects and new forms of schooling, investigates practices in schools and develops innovations in this field (see www.schooloffice-sh.de/texte/i/ipts.htm). Among other things, it contributes to the PIT-program. Although PIT-materials are self-explanatory, teachers and policemen have been educated by an expert team consisting of members of IPTS, LKA, KOSS and the psychological services for schools. So, very different professional perspectives are brought together. KOSS stands for "Koordinierungsstelle schulische Suchtvorbeugung" (Co-ordination office for the prevention of addiction in schools) in Schleswig-Holstein, an NGO closely co-operating with another NGO, LSSH (regional office for the prevention of addiction) (see www.koss-sh.de and www.lssh.de). They share an office in Kiel. LKA is part of the police authority of the federal state.

---

[14] That prison was closed in 2005 by Senator Kusch. Although my course did not survive the transfer of this institution into a department of Fuhlsbüttel, it is now adapted in Israel (Uri Timor, oral communication).

3.3 Non governmental organisations in Schleswig-Holstein

Whereas the previous category can be characterized by its close proximity to the ministries of education and the interior, respectively, and thus act officially and according to political orders, the already mentioned KOSS and LSSH and the LSV and bfw, too, are non governmental organisations which nevertheless closely cooperate with the authorities. Others like diba, Packhaus or Petze do not have this semi-official character and they are free to develop offers which are successful in the "prevention market". On the other hand, this normally implies to have fewer resources available. Some of these organisations are quite small and their impact may be restricted to single courses.

3.4 Universities in Hamburg

At the Institute of Criminological Social Research (IKS) of the University of Hamburg there is one of the rare post-graduate study programmes (in German) in criminology which leads to an M.A. degree in criminology for lawyers, social scientists, psychologists, social workers and other academics. In principle, the field of crime prevention is included, but it does not form a main focus. Furthermore, it is possible to participate in practitioners' courses consisting of certified courses in two different formats: weekly intensive courses (Studienwochen) or in a whole extra-occupational study programme (Kontaktstudium), open for nearly everyone; both of these programmes focus on varying specific topics. Especially these latter forms offer an excellent opportunity as a framework for questions related to crime prevention – even more so since these offers are conceptualised partly on demand. This seems to be a very specific solution and accessible for our target group.

There are additional opportunities in the law faculty, where crime prevention research projects have been carried out and experts act as consultants on questions of crime prevention (Klaus Sessar, Peter Wetzels).

Another university that has to be mentioned is Hamburg University of Applied Sciences (HAW) which was re-organised in 2005. The faculty of social work and care consists of about 40 professors and more than 1,200 students. Professor Jens Weidner is very active in the field of violence prevention and has developed the so-called anti-aggression and coolness training programs. At his institute of confrontative pedagogic, anti-aggression training and coolness training (Deutsches Institut für Konfrontative Pädagogik, AAT und CT, Hamburg), he is offering courses to interested persons and companies (see www.prof-Jens-Weidner.de).

The institute of social practice (ISP) affiliated with the **Protestant University of Applied Sciences, Rauhes Haus** offers an extra occupational study programme and carries out research and evaluation studies (see Möbius & Klawe 2002), develops programs and advises others on the implementation of projects. It is possible to get a B.A. in Social Work. However, I could not find out explicitly about any basic training or advanced training in crime prevention.

The new Hamburg Police College (in the process of being established since January 2007), which replaces the faculty of police of the former Fachhochschule für Öffentliche Verwaltung (FHÖV), will offer a study programme in Security Management for senior executives in the private security sector (starting in October 2007). The curriculum as it is presented on the website (www.hdp-hamburg.de, 29.7.2007) will not include any specific courses in crime prevention, except those with the objective of preventing terrorist acts. However, its main purpose is to educate policemen – this academy resembles the one in Altenholz.

Since 1 January 2006, the institute for Urban Research (Stadtforschung) has been transferred from the Technical University of Harburg to the newly founded Hafen City Universität. There was a main focus on crime prevention. Professor Breckner participated in a European study on insecurity in big cities and has served as a consultant for the Hamburg projects of "social city" which are both relevant to our subject.

Related to tertiary prevention in the form of treatment mainly for sex offenders and similar offenders with distinctive pathologic features – comparable with Kiel – the university clinic (UKE) and the forensic institution of Ochsenzoll provide aftercare, counselling, expertise and closed institutionalisation. Professor Berner acts as a consultant for the prison system.

4. Conclusion

The Beccaria project asked for an analysis of qualification offers for players in crime prevention in Schleswig-Holstein. This article has given an overview of measures, projects and initiatives which are currently in place in this northernmost federal state of Germany. The situation does not seem to be too bad. A broad and exhaustive endeavour of primary crime prevention concerning children and young people as potential offenders has been implemented in schools and sport clubs. Furthermore, local councils of crime prevention identify more focused requirements concerning this group and other dimensions like a companion for the elderly, identifying hot spots and incivilities at an early stage. The more you dig into this field, the more you can find. However, it is not clear how intensive these efforts are in practice and not at all if they are effective. I hardly found any strong evidence of activities connected with evaluation or effects. This is also true with respect to evidence that the programs provided do really offer what is required. Without any doubt the Sport against Violence project is a positive undertaking and I am convinced that young people are making use of it. But does it work in preventing right-wing extremism? How could it be proved that the youngsters joining sports clubs would otherwise turn to politically violent groups?

Another intention was to relate the crime prevention activities to the crime situation which - according to police statistics - on an overall level has developed in a favourable direction. However, my assessment of the risk of victimization of certain persons not only relied on an official appraisal but also on other sources of information. Taking the dark figure into account and the specific vulnerability or dangerousness of certain groups, crime prevention activities on the secondary and tertiary level make sense. Again, efforts to support women and children could be identified and also a certain awareness for the weakness of immigrants in encounters with neo-Nazis, but no programs which focus on handicapped people or homosexuals who have fallen victim to hate crimes. Some efforts focus on sex offenders and on the ministry level prevention of terrorism is at least verbally an important aspect. Analysing police statistics, these efforts may reflect a moral panic. From conviction statistics we can clearly derive a growing punitive attitude towards sex offenders – this is not specific for Schleswig-Holstein. A sense of punitiveness is also reflected in prevention activities concerning domestic violence (KIK).

A different approach for drawing conclusions looks more specifically at training offers by institutions and relates this to the personnel in charge of the measures, projects and initiatives. For qualification programs it is crucial to know who the people in charge of these programs are. Six different groups can be identified from the previous analysis:

- Policemen and –women
- Social workers
- Teachers
- Sport instructors, trainers
- Doctors and other medical staff
- Ordinary citizens and business people

For police officers it is clearly part of their ordinary job to deal with crime prevention and thus these questions are more or less intensively included into their training. Social work deals - among other things - with risks, deprived living conditions and deficits or vulnerability of individuals as an essential feature of its discipline. Thus crime prevention activities (should) constitute a common element of their professional skills, too. But as for teachers, serious doubts arise. It is even ambiguous whether schools and kindergartens have a mandate for educating pupils or if the first should concentrate on teaching and imparting knowledge to the children and the latter should concentrate on their supervision and educational activities. Teachers are seldom confronted with crime prevention during their training. Similar questions concern instructors and trainers in sports. The sports association of the federal state only refers to pedagogical qualifications. Medical doctors and related staff of the medical field know at least something about the general concepts of prevention. Furthermore, there is a close proximity between crime and illness in etiological concepts which are relevant to secondary and tertiary crime prevention focusing on specific delinquents.

People in charge of the local councils of crime prevention are in most cases the mayor or a police officer as the chairperson of this agency. In the first case we are dealing with experts in administration, who do not seem professionally qualified for crime prevention. The same is true for ordinary citizens. Keeping John Braithwaite's article "Thinking harder about democratising social control" (1994) in mind I appreciate this development to ground crime prevention in the life world of ordinary people, provided they acquire the necessary knowledge.

Seen from the perspective of the people who run the initiatives and projects, there seems to be an urgent need for offering courses to teachers and other educational personnel, to the responsible people in sport, to ordinary citizens and people from the administration. To what extent do the active people in local councils use the existing offers? Do the educational institutions aim at these people and what about their strategies to approach them? This task probably resembles the requirements in qualifying volunteers for aftercare of prisoners.

It must be stated that three out of six groups of activists are already prepared to some extent although not sufficiently. In this respect, the situation of police officers is probably better than that of social workers and medical staff. I would like to recommend separate courses for police officers, social workers and medical personnel because these groups already have knowledge about basic principles. Most of the existing institutions do not offer any focused trainings in crime prevention. This is within the realm of single specific courses (like the Studienwoche at the University of Hamburg) or institutes like IPTS, the anti-aggression/violence-trainings or diba. The universities concentrate more on expert counselling and developing treatment programs. If the Beccaria project is able to develop a complete study programme in crime prevention this must be highly appreciated and welcomed.

References

Braithwaite, J. (1994). "Thinking Harder About Democratising Social Control" in Alder, C. & Wundersitz, J. (eds.), Family Conferencing and Juvenile Justice: the Way Forward or Misplaced Optimism? Canberra (S. 199-216).

Bundeskriminalamt (2003). Kriminalprävention in Deutschland. Länder-Bund-Projektsammlung. [709 pages. www.bka.de]

Centre for the Prevention of Youth Crime (ed.) (2004). Prevention of Youth Crime in Germany. Educational Strategies, Trends, Experiences and Approaches. München.

Cierpka, Manfred (2002). FAUSTLOS – ein Curriculum für sozial-emotionales Lernen im Kindergarten. Heidelberg: Heidelberger Präventionszentrum.

Hagemann, Otmar (2004). "Opfer" im Blickpunkt von Strafgefangenen. in: Freiheit und Unfreiheit. Arbeit mit Straftätern innerhalb und außerhalb des Justizvollzuges, hrsg. von G. Rehn, R. Nanninga und A. Thiel (2004), Herbolzheim: Centaurus. (S. 397-421)

Hirschi, Travis (1969). Causes of Delinquency. Berkeley.

Holst, Bettina & Frommel, Monika (2004). Wirkungsweisen von KIK in Kiel 1997-2003 Internet

IPTS, Weißer Ring & Rat für Kriminalitätsverhütung (Hg.) (1996). PIT Schulische Prävention im Team, Version 2 / 97. o.O.

Kase, Gunter (2004). PIT - Prävention im Team Persönlichkeitsentwicklung und Samfund. PIT - Das Original aus Schleswig-Holstein. In: Berliner Forum Gewaltprävention, Nr. 16, 5. Jg., S. 95-102

Kase, Gunter (2005). Prävention im Team (PIT) – ein schulisches Präventionsprogramm aus Schleswig-Holstein. In: Berliner Forum Gewaltprävention, Nr. 22, 6. Jg., S. 147-149

Knauer, Raingard (2004). Prävention braucht Partizipation. Anforderungen an Prävention aus der Sicht der Jugendhilfe. In: Ostendorf 2004, 35-42

Koller, Frank & Hagemann, Otmar (2007). Zufriedenheit mit dem Täter-Opfer-Ausgleich. In: Zeitschrift für soziale Strafrechtspflege Nr. 43, 17. Jg., S. 55-57

Korn, Judy & Heitmann, Helmut (o.J.). Verantwortung übernehmen – Abschied von Hass und Gewalt. Berlin.

Landesregierung Schleswig-Holstein (Hrsg.) (2004). Periodischer SicherheitsBericht Schleswig-Holstein 1994-2003. Kiel.

Möbius, Thomas & Klawe, Willy (Hrsg.) (2002). AIB – Ambulante Intensive Betreuung. Handbuch für eine innovative Praxis in der Jugendhilfe.

Morris, Allison & Maxwell, Gabrielle (eds.) (2001): Restorative Justice for Juveniles. Conferencing, Mediation and Circles. Oxford & Portland.

Ostendorf, Heribert (1997). Jugendgerichtsgesetz. Kommentar. 4. völlig überarbeitete Auflage. Köln u.a.

Ostendorf, Heribert (ed.) (2004). Effizienz von Kriminalprävention. Erfahrungen im Ostseeraum.

Pötzke, Klaus Michael (2006). Sport gegen Gewalt, Intoleranz und Fremdenfeindlichkeit. In: Kerner, H.-J. & Marks, E. (Hrsg.), Internetdokumentation des Deutschen Präventionstages Hannover.
www.praeventionstag.de/content/11_praev/doku/poetzke/index_11_poetzke.html

PSB [Zweiter Periodischer Sicherheitsbericht] (2006). (second Periodic Report on Security) hrsg. von den Bundesministerien des Innern und der Justiz. Paderborn.

Rat für Kriminalitätsverhütung Schleswig-Holstein(2001). Konzept für Kriminalitätsverhütung. Straffälligenhilfe. Aug. 2001

Rat für Kriminalitätsverhütung in Schleswig-Holstein (2003). Kriminalprävention in Stadtteilen. Kriminalitätsverhütung durch Interaktion. Institutionalisierung, Konzeption, Beispiele, Empfehlungen. Kiel

Schäfer, Heiner (2004). "Young Russians" in Germany. Immigrants lost between their origin and future? In: Centre for the Prevention of Crime Youth Crime (ed.), Prevention of Youth Crime in Germany. München. S. 61-98

Schleswig-Holsteinischer Landtag, 15. Wahlperiode, Drucksache 15/1499 vom 10.1.2002: Bericht der Landesregierung Angebote der Prävention bei Kindern und Jugendlichen in Schleswig-Holstein

Strang, Heather & Braithwaite, John (eds.) (2000): Restorative Justice. Philosophy to practice. Aldershot u.a.: Ashgate.

Trauernicht, Gitta (2005). Vernachlässigung von Kindern vorbeugen – Früherkennungsuntersuchungen zur Pflicht machen und soziale Frühwarnsysteme entwickeln: Startschuss für Schleswig-Holstein. Rede am 28.11.2005 in Kiel [über Schutzengel für SH]

Wetzels, Peter (1997). Gewalterfahrungen in der Kindheit. Sexueller Missbrauch, körperliche Misshandlung und deren langfristige Konsequenzen. Baden-Baden: Nomos

Witte, Matthias D. & Sander, Uwe (Hrsg.) (2006). Erziehungsresistent? "Problemjugendliche" als besondere Herausforderung für die Jugendhilfe. Schneider-Verlag.

Jim Hilborn, Anu Leps

Status Report Estonia - The Development of Crime Prevention Education in Estonia

We have argued that crime prevention in Estonia is still quite tentative and uncertain. There are neither a few clear policy directives nor is there any real commitment of resources to the development of crime prevention. In this paper we are advocating the development of crime prevention education to properly prepare crime prevention practitioners.

History

There have been some efforts at university level including the following:

- In 2005: training module "Crime prevention - theoretical foundations and practical tools" at Tallinn University for Social Work MA studies (2 CP);
- In 2006 and 2007: training module "Risk assessment and crime prevention" at Tartu University for Social Work BA and MA studies (2 CP).
- In 2006: lectures at Tallinn University about CPTED for MA students of Urban Studies.

These lectures looked at:

- Defining crime prevention, crime reduction, community safety, different strategic documents (UN, UE, etc);
- History of the CP since 10,000 BCE;
- Methods – the problem analysis triangle, the conjunction of criminal opportunity, 5Is, SMART etc.;
- Evidence of successful crime prevention programs.

In terms of resources in Estonian, there are now the following:
In 2006, the manual "Become a Problem Solving Crime Analyst in 55 small steps" (Clarke & Eck, 2003) was translated (Probleemikeskseks kriminaalanalüütikuks: 55 lihtsa sammuga) by the Academy for Civil Defence in collaboration with the Estonian police.

In 2007 "The Concerned Citizens Guide to Crime Prevention and Community Safety: A First look at the Complex Issue of Crime Prevention Planning" (Hilborn & Hilborn) was prepared and translated with support from the Ministry of Justice. It is now in press.

Together these two books provide a good theoretical basis for crime prevention education in Estonian. The Ministry of Justice and the NGO *Baltic Crime Prevention Practitioners Association* also have good collections of crime prevention material in English.

However, at present we do not have a proper Criminology Department, nor do we have a Crime Prevention program at any University in Estonia. Establishing such a program is one of our key objectives. The closest that we have come at present is the course at Tallinn Pedagogical College. Since 2002, Helgi Hilborn has been offering a course in crime prevention for students of Social Work. Helgi Hilborn also translated "The Concerned Citizens Guide". Marcus Felson gave a lecture on situational crime prevention in the fall of 2006. Though the quality of this course is quite good, it is not being offered at university level.

Anu Leps has been active in the promotion of crime prevention. She was the Estonian representative in the EU project "Crime Opportunity Profiling of Streets" (COPS), running from 2003 to 2007. Anu Leps is also the Estonian representative for the European Crime Prevention Network (EUCPN). Jim Hilborn secured Canadian funding for a small group to visit Canada in February 2005 to look at crime prevention practices. The group met with staff from the International Centre for Crime Prevention (ICPC), the National Crime Prevention Centre, Correctional Services Canada, Peel Regional Police, and the Ontario Criminal Justice Training Centre.

Also, an NGO, the Baltic Crime Prevention Practitioners Association (BCPPA), was established in 2005. This NGO works as a partner with the Estonian Ministry of Justice. The BCPPA's mission is:

- To promote the development and application of evidence-based crime prevention policy and practice in Estonia, the Baltics, and the rest of the European Union;
- To support the development of crime prevention practitioners by producing books, training materials, and offering workshops and seminars.
- To collaborate with crime prevention practitioners, NGOs, educational facilities, and government agencies in the EU and internationally in order to develop crime prevention both as a profession and also as a new discipline that draws upon criminology, law and related urban planning professions.

In addition to lectures at different educational facilities and training courses in the Northern Police Prefecture in Tallinn on problem-oriented policing, the main accomplishment of the BCPPA has been the "Concerned Citizen's Guide" (2007). The BCPPA is planning further publications for the future.

Given the limited human and financial resources available for the development of crime prevention education in Estonia, we feel that our progress has been reasonable but we need to do a lot more.

Our Vision of Crime Prevention

In the development of crime prevention in Estonia we have drawn heavily on the work done in the UK, Canada and the USA. We are also active members of the first Beccaria project. As a starting point we are using Paul Ekblom's most recent definition of crime prevention:

Reducing the risk of criminal events in terms of their probability of occurrence and consequent harm, by intervening in their causes

Although we agree with Schneider and Kitchen that *fear of crime* and *crime* are separate issues - even though they are related phenomena - we also believe that crime prevention practitioners must consider not only the impact of their interventions on crime and disorder but also the impact of crime prevention interventions on people's fear of crime and the overall quality of their social life.

Thus crime prevention education must also look at a wider range of issues related to harm, community safety and the social health of the community. This aspect of crime prevention planning and education is caught by Paul Ekblom in his discussions around community safety. He has written that

Community safety focuses less on individual criminal and disorderly events and more on consequences of crime and disorder as a whole; hence the goal is harm reduction and the delivery of a range of social and economic benefits rather than merely lowering the numbers of events or reducing their rate of growth. Community safety is an aspect of the **quality of life**, a state of existence in which people, individually, collectively and in organisations, and in public and private space, enjoy the following conditions:

freedom from and/or reassurance about a range of real and perceived risks centring on crime, antisocial behaviour, disorder and drug dealing and abuse
ability to cope with the consequences of those incidents that they nevertheless experience, at reasonable cost (e.g. without curtailment of going out)
help to cope if unable to do so alone, whether informally from the community, or more formally by for example victim support or insurance
confidence that the police, CJS and other agencies will, if needed, provide a responsive, fair and effective service that delivers justice and remedies to the problems they experience or risks they perceive
trust – within and across cultural boundaries – in neighbours, colleagues and passers-by to support them both morally and materially in terms of sympathy, collectively-upheld moral order, social control and support
When all these conditions are met to a sufficient degree, they enable individuals, families and, communities to:
- pursue the necessities of their cultural, social and economic life;
- to receive adequate services;
- to exercise their skills;

- to enjoy well-being;
- to engage in community life
- and to create wealth in the widest sense.

Community safety and the issue of harm are quite problematic. But so is the whole area of criminology and law. This is a contested policy area. We want the students in crime prevention education to struggle with such problems. If instead of speaking of crime prevention and community safety, the discussion is about harm reduction and social health promotion, then the policy debate becomes much broader. When Paul Ekblom adds harm to his definition of crime prevention, he is trying to expand the boundaries. In the same way, the Centre for Crime and Justice Studies in the UK has a Harm and Society project[15] to stimulate debate about the limitations of criminal justice and promote alternative perspectives on social harm, crime and social policy. It seeks to change the terms of the debate by working with others to catalyse a fundamental shift in social and criminal justice policy. We believe that such a change would help in the development of crime prevention in Estonia.

Crime Prevention: Interdisciplinary and Multi-Sectoral
Crime prevention is more than the sum of its parts. C. Ray Jeffery coined the term "crime prevention through environmental design" in 1977[16]. In his CPTED model he argued that criminology must be an interdisciplinary science involving the **biological and behavioural sciences** (biology, psychology, psychiatry, sociology, political science, economics, and anthropology) and the **policy sciences** (criminal law, public administration, philosophy, ethics, and history)[17]. More recently, Anthony Bottoms argued that criminologists need to draw upon "the town planner's views, the demographer's views, and the ordinary person's everyday experience of the city...to get to grips with issues relating to cities and crime"[18]. Bottoms' insight is certainly true for the crime prevention profession.

Thus, in addition to Jeffery's emphasis on the biological and behavioural sciences (or the social cognitive neurosciences) and the policy sciences, crime prevention must add the **planning and design professions** (urban designers, planners, architects, engineers) as well as those professionals active **in harm reduction** and **health promotion**. The crime prevention practitioner must also be sensitive to **political trends**, the impact of the **media** and the **community's fears and concerns**. The exact relationship of these diverse strands is often contested but together these different parts make up the policy and practice of crime prevention.

---

[15] http://www.crimeandjustice.org.uk/harmandsocproject.html

[16] C. Ray Jeffery (1977). Crime Prevention through Environmental Design, Sage Publications, Inc., London.

[17] C.Ray Jeffery (1990). Criminology An Interdisciplinary Approach, Prentic Hall, Englewood Cliffs, New Jersey.

[18] Anthony E. Bottoms (2007). "Place, Space ,Crime, and Disorder", in Maguire, M., Morgan, R. Reiner, R. (editors), The Oxford Handbook of Criminology, 4th Edition. Oxford University Press, New York.

Crime prevention is a profession that focuses on the **participatory** planning and design of the social and built environment as much as it is about either criminology or the law. If criminology is an interdisciplinary science, then crime prevention is a multi-sectoral profession whose scope goes into broad issues of harm, community safety and the quality of the social life as it actively engages the public and those professions who have not traditionally been that interested in issues of crime and criminology.

The crime prevention practitioner must have an operational level of understanding and competency in the:
- The social cognitive neurosciences,
- The policy sciences, and
- The planning and design professions.

Specialized technical skills in **crime analysis, crime mapping** and **community mobilization** also have to be included. Like planning in general, crime prevention is place-specific. It is all "about trying to manage change in places or localities for the benefit of citizens and their users. The cutting edge of planning can usually at the end of the day be reduced to a simple question: 'What do we do here?'[19]

Need for Balance

Paul Ekblom has argued that the present weighing is unbalanced with too much emphasis being placed on issues of management and maintenance – police and criminal justice-reaction - and not enough on earlier efforts at design and planning.

---

[19] Ted Kitchen (2007). Skills for Planning Practice, Palgrave Macmillan, New York.

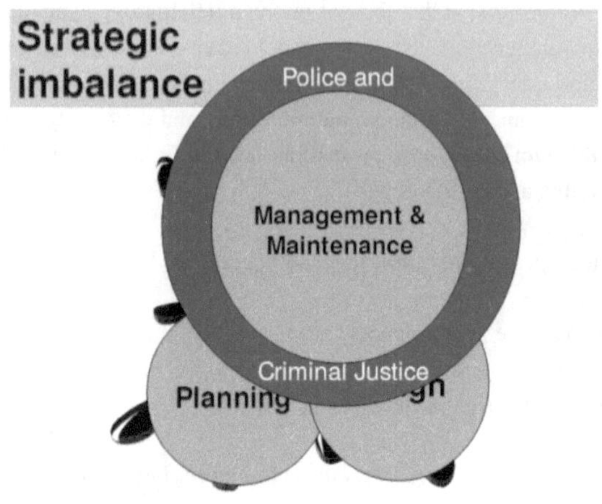

When he believes the balance should be more

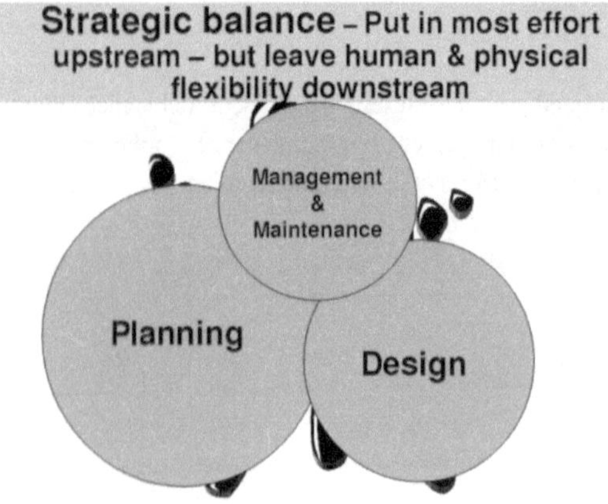

We agree with him since our model of crime prevention practice has more to do with planning and design than with the criminal justice system's traditional reaction to crime and disorder.

The Future Remains Uncertain
We believe in our vision of crime prevention and that there is a need for adequate and specialized crime prevention education. At present there is no political consensus on this approach, nor have we found the necessary resources. But there is always hope.

Michel Marcus

Status Report France - The 'Prevention-Safety Project Managers' and their Training in France[20]

Some points of reference:
- Various denominations are used to designate the people in charge of questions of prevention and safety. The choice of denomination depends on the orientation which the collective intends to give to this role;
- The circular of 4 December 2006 on the new generation of Local Safety Contracts, emphasises the necessity of training the coordinators with regard to crime prevention;
- One must bear in mind that the recruitment of a coordinator is left to the discretion of elected representatives and therefore not an obligation for the latter.

The rapid development of prevention-safety project managers, which has followed numerous public safety policy developments, incites one to ask whether this has assisted in the creation of a new professional space and therefore an occupation. To pose such a question inevitably comes back to looking into the efforts that are, or are not provided, regarding training in the construction of such a professional field.[21]

By profession, one refers to:
-The possession of specialised knowledge;
-The exercise of a monopoly on a branch of industry;
-The control of access to the organisation. The occupation would therefore be defined as the daily exercise of a professional activity with its own categories of action and specific codes of interpretation. This said, it would be the practical exercise of a profession, understood in the sense of a common culture based on knowledge and know-how.

Taking into account such a definition, to what extent do the 'prevention-safety project managers' represent a profession and thus consequently an occupation? How does one construct such a professional field? What is the role and weight of training in this field?

---

[20] No denomination is neutral. The choice of 'Prevention-safety Project Manager' seemed to be the least prone to controversy.

[21] See « Origines, Trajectoires et profils des chargés de mission prévention-sécurité » in Les Cahiers de la sécurité, n° 58, 2005.

Did it anticipate the developments of the occupation or has it just been adapted to them?

Indeed, it is important to retrace the process of the institutionalisation of a profession. This process starts with pioneering experiments, which if relevant, are diffused in the areas where they have meaning. In the field that interests us, this first phase opens with the creation of the Community Councils of Crime Prevention in 1983, following the urban riots of Vénissieux. Following on from there in 1997 Local Safety Contracts were created and, in 2002, the Local Councils of Safety and Crime Prevention. These new initiatives will see the emergence of new actors who are the 'prevention-safety project managers'. In this spirit, a first training effort has been implemented to structure the new activity. Thus the French Forum for Urban Safety (FFSU) and the Institute of High Studies for Interior Security (IHESI currently IN-HES) will try to provide a frame of reference and a common basis of knowledge to these new actors through training sessions, seminars, colloquiums or network meetings.

The dissemination of these new players in the area will involve a phase of supervision coming from the normalisation of procedures and production of a public discussion which increases the value of the activity. This phase is often that of legislative developments which try to better define a role and to frame an activity (the last to date is the Law relating to the Prevention of Crime).

This therefore opens a process of identity construction which expresses itself through the construction of a professional field. Selection procedures, based on the integration of rituals of constituted codes and knowledge, are therefore implemented. This demarcation of the field, which aims at gathering values around a vision of the world and around techniques, will therefore be done by means of training.

Moreover, in the case of the 'prevention-safety project managers', it is a particular process of institutionalisation as they are dependent on the institutions which create the conditions for the emergence of this practice and control its development. From that moment onwards, the division of this field of activity between institutions of various configurations and actors of multiple profiles, limits the feeling of belonging to a professional unit and makes the implementation of training difficult. Thus, the question of the construction of a common culture, and therefore a common identity, arises.

The term *construction of an identity* also means a process of integration and federation of the members of a group around common values, but at the same time the demarcation of an activity which asserts their own competences. The first gives its members the capacity to recognise themselves as part of a group, to attain a principle of membership despite the geographical and statutory splitting of jobs. The second assumes the occupation of a position and the control of specific techniques. This identity, in its double dimension, depends on three essential criteria which play a part in the legitimization of this activity:

- The transparency of their action: the increase in the number of activities reserved for them, which depend on the configuration of the collective (intercommunality or not, the community having a city policy of priority zones or not, such as Sensitive Urban Zones-ZUS- or a priority zone in the eyes of national education such as Priority Education Zones-ZEP-) does not always favour this transparency. This lack of transparency prevents the definition of only one training profile of these 'prevention-safety project managers' as 'transversality' seems to be the essential theme of their activity.

- The visibility of their activities: the diversity of their denomination and the competences that they attribute to this job title, but also to their position in the local organisational chart (diversity of their status: territorially or contractually linked) can or cannot work in favour of a better visibility of their actions. This visibility is also strongly linked to the support of the institution extended to the project manager.

- The construction of a common culture based on a specific basis of knowledge having vocation to guarantee their professionalisation. Indeed, the construction of a professional field based on sharing a common culture and corroborating professional interests is not yet accomplished. On the contrary, the project managers appear to be a divided professional unit, made up of relatively isolated individuals due to the diversity of their career. The difficulty of narrowing down their field of competence, which is defined by the institutions according to their legislative needs and developments, prevents training bodies from anticipating new directions of the trade and obliges them to provide them with more reactive training. This is without a doubt the most problematic aspect, which we will explore further.

Indeed, it is difficult to have an overall picture of the prevention-safety project managers' careers because of the difficulty of homogenizing their activities. Two categorisation criteria can be retained. The first concerns the form of their individual course:

- **Initial training** whose recipients are often those who have made the choice to specialise in prevention and safety quite early on. This course can be long or short (from 2 to 5 years). This initial training is characterised by diplomas which are already very specialised (university degrees, professional diplomas) and by other diplomas, which are without doubt more numerous, conceived as a subset of broader training in political science, local public action, public policy, law, sociology of organisations etc.. (for example, Master of Political Science speciality Risk Management). This second scenario points out the deficiencies of these training courses, which are more a 'sensitisation' towards questions of prevention and safety than real training programmes.

- **Continuous training** whose recipients are generally already in a professional environment and would like to acquire new competences that allow them to exercise new functions. There are fewer of such trainings and their content concerns methodological aspects.

The second criterion concerns the content. What are knowledge and know-how to a prevention-safety project manager?

Three aspects appear to be important:

- The expertise of a specific knowledge linked to prevention and safety. This occurs through knowledge of the development of public safety policies and the different initiatives attached to them: city policy, territorial stakes linked to these policies (good knowledge of local dynamics), knowledge of actors and their logics.

It is increasingly important to have a transversal knowledge which must be integrated in the training.

- -The acquisition of the practice of several languages, to understand and to render understanding of them among all those involved - Police, Justice, National Education. This point is important when one knows the place of the partnership within local public prevention policies which involve the comprehension of the logics of partnership but also those of the different institutions;
- The capacity to support exchanges between players employing differing modes of intervention (to enable different players to talk and work together within their own logic). It makes reference to the necessity of breaking with the spirit of certain institutions.

Taking into account these expectations, what responses are there with regard to training? The proposed training courses can be divided into three large fields. We should keep in mind that the categorisation presented is not exhaustive but represents a large part of the training market open to these actors:

Local public policies: this category regroups all the training sessions dealing with the management of territorial collectives, local public administration, management of conflict in public spaces, territorial public action. At the same time it gives access to a good knowledge of public policies but also of the French political and administrative system.

The management and evaluation of risks: this is without doubt the most technical category as it aims to train, according to diplomas, general practitioners or safety specialists. In both cases, the programs are structured around risk and crisis management.

Criminology: this is a category that is also highly specialised as it deals with questions related to the police and their methods of investigation, questions of punishment, and focuses on a better understanding of crime and its perpetrators. In this domain, not enough French degrees exist in comparison to those that one can find in other countries such as Canada or Belgium.

Local public policy and public institutions	**Management and evaluation of risks**
Master in Management of Territorial Collectives (Nanterre)	Master in Risk Management (Nanterre)
Master in Local Public Administration (Lille)	Master in Risk Engineering (Paris 5)
University Degree Policies and Initiatives of Territorial Safety (Paris 5)	Master in Global Risk and Crisis Management (Sorbonne)
Master in Police, Safety, Society (Toulouse)	Master in Decision and Risk Management (Lyon)
Master in Law and Safety Policies (Saint-Cyr-au-Mont-d'Or)	Professional Diploma in Risk Management (Avignon)
Master in Urban Safety in France and Europe (Dijon)	
Master in Military History and Safety Policy (IEP Aix in partnership with the CNFPT[22])	

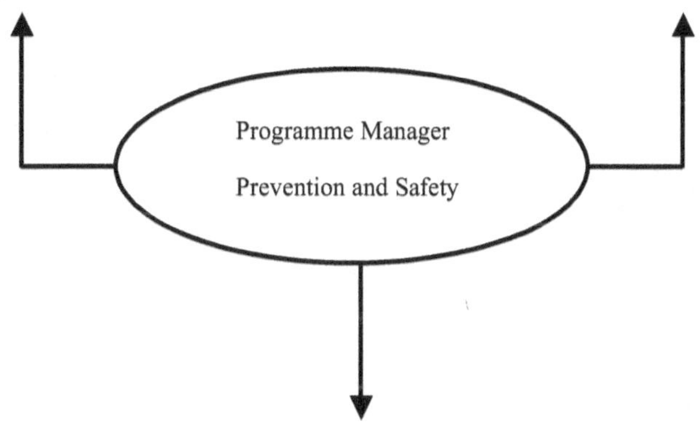

Criminology
University Degrees in Criminology (Nancy, Rennes, Grenoble) Master in Criminology (Rennes)

---

[22] Institute of Political Studies (IEP), National Centre for the Public Territorial Function (CNFPT).

Besides these classic training sessions, organisations such as the French Forum for Urban Safety have launched training programs for 'prevention-safety project managers'. Indeed, convinced that the project manager is the essential element and the carrier of a local safety policy, for several years the French Forum for Urban Safety has been organising cycles of supplementary training sessions intended to enrich the practice of these actors and local policies in general. In the same way, the European Forum for Urban Safety (FESU) has entered a partnership with the University of Bourgogne and the city of Dijon in the form of a professional Master's programme entitled 'Urban Safety in France and Europe' whose objective is to support an exchange of experiences likely to enrich the basis of knowledge of these new safety actors. It is the Institute of Political Studies (IEP), National Centre for the Public Territorial Function (CNFPT) currently exploring paths to link up various existing programs and coordinate nationally-based initiatives. It is in this context that the Forum participates with enthusiasm in the Beccaria project.

Lode Walgrave, Dieter Burssens, Elmar Weitekamp

Status Report Belgium - Training Programmes in Crime Prevention in Belgium

This survey is limited to training programmes focusing on the prevention of crime in the strict sense of the word. They mostly regard variations of technical or situational prevention. Excluded are the many initiatives of prevention through social work, early intervention etc.

In Belgium, the distribution of competencies between the federal state and the three communities leads to a relatively clear distribution of responsibilities regarding prevention[23]. The Federal Government, and especially the Ministry of the Interior, is responsible for police and public safety. The major part of the direct crime prevention initiatives depends on this Ministry. Under the auspices of the Ministry of the Interior, some municipalities and pro-vinces take local prevention initiatives in this regard.

The communities are competent on what the Belgian Law calls "personalizable matters", meaning education, culture and welfare. Almost all initiatives trying to prevent crime indirectly through welfare-promoting initiatives belong to this group.

An exception here may be several drugs programmes, a part of which is organised also with the support of the federal government. But as they address already registered drug users, these programmes should in fact be considered more as treatment programmes than as prevention programmes.

There is no general agency to coordinate all prevention initiatives at the level of the Ministry of Interior.

The Federal Police, Directory for Training, organizes specialized training programmes. Recent programmes are:
- Protection of public buildings

The programme of two days addresses the 'techno-preventive advisers'[24].

The subjects are: technical preventive measures, fire protection, electronic protection through access control and surveillance cameras, protection of art, and some concrete examples.

---

[23] In its complicated politico-administrative structure, Belgium is divided into three 'regions' (Flanders, Brussels, and Wallonia), with autonomous competencies focussed on economics and labour, and into three 'communities' (Flanders, including the Dutch-speaking population in Brussels; the French community in Belgium, including the French-speaking population in Brussels; a smaller German community), whose competencies concern especially welfare, education and culture. The federal state still holds important responsibilities, for example in the fields of defence, foreign affairs, social safety, justice, police and public safety.

[24] Advisers on technical prevention are specialized staff, appointed by municipalities.

- Protection of City Halls

The one-day programme is addressed to the persons responsible for safety of city halls.

The subjects are comparable to the above programme, but a special topic on protecting documents is added.

- Car crime

The one-day programme is addressed to advisers on technical prevention.

The bigger cities and the provinces occasionally organize comparable programmes.

Initiatives with regard to private and special safety are ruled under the **Act of 10 April 1990 on Private and Special Safety**, updated several times till 27 December 2006.

This act rules among other things the activities of private companies concerning safety advice. These are persons or companies that deliver services or extend advice in order to prevent criminal acts against people or property.

All such companies must get a formal homologate on by the Ministry of the Interior. On 17 January 2007, almost 300 such people or companies were recognized. They range from very small one-man businesses to big international companies.

One of the biggest in Belgium is Crime Control, with currently 35 members of staff, operating in Belgium, the Netherlands, France and Germany. They advise on technical safety problems, do private internal investigations, organize trainings, publish handbooks, etc.

Many of the recognized agencies for safety advice set up short training programmes, focused on concrete safety problems or threats.

These include, for example
- Coping with aggression: a programme for pharmacists, and including role-playing;
- How to behave during a bank robbery: a programme for bank employees, including role-playing;
- Technical prevention of burglary: for police officers who will give advice to private citizens;
- Prevention of car theft: for taxi companies;
- Prevention of internal theft: for staff members of department stores
- Recognizing fraud attempts: for antique dealers.

More atypical is a recent initiative taken by **TPO (Team Preventie Ontwikkeling** – Team for the development of prevention). TPO groups include academics and advanced practitioners, and aim at developing "desirable prevention". They hope to develop a more balanced view on crime prevention, where direct crime-focused prevention programmes, based mainly on situ ational and other defensive approaches would at least be completed by more comprehensive, more socially emancipatory approaches to crime and insecurity.

Concrete training programmes are being prepared.